MW00617187

Tsunami
A Report from Phi Phi Island

Studies in Austrian Literature, Culture and Thought
Translation Series

General Editors:

Jorun B. Johns
Richard H. Lawson

Josef Haslinger

Tsunami

A Report from Phi Phi Island

Translated by Thomas S. Hansen
and
Abby J. Hansen

Afterword by
Thomas S. Hansen

ARIADNE PRESS
Riverside, California

Ariadne Press would like to express its appreciation to the Bundesministerium für Unterricht, Kunst und Kultur for assistance in publishing this book.

.KUNST

Translated from the German
Phi Phi Island. Ein Bericht
© S. Fischer Verlag GmbH, Frankfurt am Main. 2007

Library of Congress Cataloging-in-Publication Data

Haslinger, Josef, 1955-
   [Phi Phi Island : ein Bericht. English.]
   Tsunami : a report from Phi Phi island / Josef Haslinger ; translated by Thomas S. Hansen and Abby J. Hansen, afterword by Thomas S. Hansen.
      p. cm. -- (Studies in Austrian literature, culture and thought. Translation series.)
   ISBN 978-1-57241-176-0
   1. Haslinger, Josef, 1955--Travel--Thailand--Phi Phi Islands. 2. Indian Ocean Tsunami, 2004. 3. Tsunamis--Thailand--Phi Phi Islands. 4. Phi Phi Islands (Thailand)--Environmental conditions. 5. Phi Phi Islands (Thailand)--Description and travel. I. Hansen, Thomas S. (Thomas Svend), 1947- II. Hansen, Abby J., 1945- III. Title.
   PT2668.A7447P55 2011
   959.3--dc22

                                                  2011011351

Cover Design
George McGinnis

Copyright 2011
by Ariadne Press
270 Goins Court
Riverside, CA 92507

All rights reserved.
No part of this publication may be reproduced or transmitted in any form or by any means without formal permission.
Printed in the United States of America.
ISBN 978-1-57241-176-0

for edith, sophie, and elias.
in memory of the victims of the
tidal wave of december 26, 2004

1

for a couple of months i was pretty sure i would never write this book. if only because i was often asked about it. you're not working on a tsunami book, are you? no, don't worry. or, man, what you went through there; guess you're not worried about what your next book's going to be! those were awkward situations. i wanted to write about it, but at the same time, i didn't. i couldn't process what i'd been through, couldn't see it from the outside. it was like a knot deep inside that i couldn't untie.

the tsunami of december 26, 2004 and its devastating effects remained a media topic for months. i saw the pictures, read the many eye-witness accounts, and, when asked, told people what had happened to us. admittedly, during every interview i would say to myself, if the tsunami question comes up, don't fall for it. you survived, and you didn't lose any family. why not just be happy and keep your mouth shut? then the conversation would turn to the tsunami, and i realized i needed to talk about it.

in the course of this, a strange blur set in. it was always just details that came to mind, images that had stuck in my memory but clouded my view of these couple of days rather than focusing it. the images clustered around two events that related only outwardly to the tsunami, events that could have happened under very different circumstances: around the one time when i suddenly felt sure i would not survive, and around the other when it looked as though we had lost both our children.

my memory of the tidal wave was a barrier. i wanted to get past it, but there didn't seem to be any way. the past lay behind me and at the same time in front of me. it surrounded me.

i had envisioned a year of writing and begun to give some thought to a new novel. but i couldn't get started. no matter what character i tried to develop, its main purpose seemed to be dealing with what i myself needed to work through. for a while i stuck to the resolution not to write directly about myself, but to treat the story like literature – as though there were something indecent about reporting on those chance occurrences that seemed to take one person's life and spare another's.

that strategy was too transparent. instead of projecting myself into other characters, i felt the urge to return to the scene of the event and reconstruct the course of the catastrophe. thus, the project turned into a report about a brief segment of my own life. soon after i had begun to work, i found it was again possible to write other texts.

tales of a person's travels to a distant land and encounters with surprises that make it uncertain whether he will survive are called adventure stories. they are often written in the first person. when someone like kara ben nemsi tells his own story, we know from the start that things will be fine in the end. i made the chance acquaintance of an adventure story.

my report in one sentence: four of us traveled to a resort on the thai island koh phi phi, and two days later all that remained of the place was the administration building, the swimming pool, and the roof of the dining pavilion, still resting on its eight concrete pillars. the one hundred and ten bungalows, two of which we had rented, had disappeared.

this is essentially the story of many tsunami survivors who were lucky enough to be spared the worst. even if they were injured and left without money, papers, and luggage, their loss cannot be compared to those who lost families and all they owned. we were the lucky survivors, but this luck left such a bitter aftertaste that it took me a long time to appreciate it. for quite a while, whenever i talked about the tsunami, my eyes would fill with tears.

the memory of having survived an immense catastrophe by pure chance follows its own logic. you can say over and over what good fortune you had, but that doesn't cover it. more than anything else, it's a memory of terror.

when i first began to grasp our good luck, edith and i were clinging to a ledge where the water had swept us, and trying to tell people who were moving from those who weren't moving anymore. those like us, who could move, were searching for family and friends. as they began to notice the corpses lying around or protruding from the debris, they started to scream or cry, or stared blankly into space.

three quarters of a year later i got a message from magdalena, a young woman who had been staying with her boyfriend in the same hotel as we were, the phi phi princess. she and her boyfriend had seen us at breakfast. she was very relieved to find out through the media that the haslingers were still alive. she felt a need to get in touch with those people she had thought about so much without actually knowing them.

we met at the christmas market in the city of steyr. her boyfriend didn't want to come along. from the outset, magdalena said, he hadn't wanted to talk with anyone – even her – about what we had all lived through. he was completely convinced that he could just forget the days between the 26th of december, 2004, and the first of january, 2005, the day they returned to austria.

it was different with her, she said as we drank mulled wine. in the first months, when everybody was talking about the tsunami, she herself couldn't talk about it. only later did she feel the need to describe it. by then nobody was interested anymore; she and her tsunami were just getting on everybody's nerves.

i said we would found a tsunami survivors' club and every year at the annual meeting tell the most harrowing tsunami stories. we would exchange tsunami videos and put the most graphic pictures of victims up on a website.

despite the mulled wine it was hard to keep up the irony. we didn't have to tell ourselves how it looked, this strange world we had entered. we talked about what we did when the water came and how we had acted when it unexpectedly turned dangerous. we talked about the hours that followed.

magdalena had broken her ankle. her boyfriend took her on his back and carried her through the ravaged landscape. they met a man with a gaping hole below his shoulder, through which you could look into his chest cavity. that is one of the few images she could remember from the scene. later, as she was being carried up a mountain path, the group had already grown to about ten people, among them a frenchman who was missing the toes on his right foot. bungalows lined the path. one looked empty. they broke into it and took shelter there. but the bungalow wasn't empty. there were the personal effects of other vacationers who never came back. the next day magdalena's boyfriend carried her back through the debris to the tennis court in front of the cabana hotel where a helicopter had landed. on board this helicopter was a reporter from epa, the european press photo agency. he took a picture of a man making his way through a garbage-strewn landscape with a woman slung on his back. a day later this photo appeared in an austrian daily newspaper, so magdalena's parents knew their daughter was alive even before she could contact them.

our relatives kept an all-night vigil in front of german television broadcasts – austrian television didn't seem to have grasped the magnitude of the catastrophe yet – and wrote us desperate text messages and emails that received no answers. there was a moment of reassurance – people finding out via the austrian foreign ministry hotline, where young military troops were helping out, that koh phi phi had not been affected by the tidal wave. the mood then swung to the opposite pole when one of my brothers, who had visited thailand frequently, researched the location of our hotel and stumbled on the information that it had been completely destroyed. before we had a chance to phone, our relatives felt such hopelessness that they were seriously discussing where to bury our bodies – should they ever be returned. and then the call came, which for so many others never materialized. we could not leave the island, but we also did not want to live among the dead. a lot of people who could move spent their time separating the living from the corpses and keeping them apart. when the final judgment was complete, half the guests staying at the phi phi princess found themselves on the side of the living. the rest were removed and covered. we survivors of koh phi phi were a random selection. the chances of survival stood at fifty-fifty in our hotel, yet the final judgment lacked any sense of justice. our family arrived and departed as a party of four.

2

koh phi phi don and koh phi phi leh, two little islands known in international parlance as the phi phi islands, are approximately forty kilometers from krabi and phuket. there are four more phi phi islands, which have never attained international fame but are highly prized by divers. only phi phi don is inhabited. the neighboring island phi phi leh, where the drop-out movie the beach with leonardo di caprio was filmed, can be reached from phi phi don in twenty minutes by sight-seeing boat. both of these islands with their rugged chalk cliffs, white sand beaches, and crystal-clear lagoons, have become the premier thailand getaway for adventurous young travelers the world over.

the tourist infrastructure – with resorts, travel agencies, scuba diving schools, and everything that can be sold to youthful vacationers – was concentrated on koh phi phi don, particularly on the narrowest part of the island, where the beaches of two facing bays come so close together that they almost merge. the jungle begins on each side of the land bridge that they form. above that, steep cliffs stretch to the sky.

on the southern bay, ton sai bay, there was a concrete jetty, built so that larger freight and excursion boats could dock. the northern bay, lohdalum, was primarily a large bathing beach with hotel bungalows, bars, and restaurants. right in the middle of this double bay, on the lowest and narrowest point of the island, where the two beaches lay closest to each other, was the most exquisite resort: the phi phi princess. here and in the neighboring cabana hotel, young people mixed with older guests who felt drawn to youth culture.

before the tsunami, phi phi island was the most publicized place on the andaman sea in thailand. from december to march every bungalow and hotel room was filled, mostly with young tourists. this narrow strip of land lying just barely above sea level was crammed with hotels, restaurants, souvenir shops, bars, diving schools, food vendors, internet cafés, rock-climbing schools, banks, and massage parlors. along with masses of tourists, money flowed to phi phi island and was distributed among thousands of people in the service sector, most of them thai. but there were also a lot of waiters, bartenders, and diving teachers who had come from the cold countries and begun a new and, often for them, their first real, life. some were freaks who made ends meet with the most wildly miscellaneous assortment of evening entertainment. others were nature-worshipers, held captive by the island's charm; still others were active in the thriving sector of the scuba diving businesses, which on phi phi island were generally still in the hands of small-time entrepreneurs devoted to the sport. at night they would meet in nearby bars and dance clubs, in the hippies bar, at carlito's, or in the reggae bar to see the fire jugglers compete, watch soccer on tv, dance, and drink whisky and cola. no matter where in the world the people came from who streamed to this place, here they behaved like a family. phi phi island was party central, a youth high. for years environmentalists have held up this slender land strip of koh phi phi don as an example of the destruction of an intact ecology. the island was in danger of consuming its entire water supply. in 1983 the thai government placed the phi phi islands under environmental protection. for phi phi leh, the law came just in time. it has remained uninhabited, even though it has become a desirable tourist destination because of its fantastic lagoon and extensive network of caves. the caves, a labyrinth with hundreds of passages and chambers up to eighty meters high, are covered with a thick layer of guano. the inhabitants are bats and cave swifts. year after year the thai government auctions harvesting rights for the swifts' nests. the license-holders, for their part, assemble teams, often their whole families, which collect the birds' nests from the stalactites at daredevil heights on scaffolding made of bamboo rods lashed together with vines. the nests are soaked, rinsed, and sold to china as a special delicacy. the strands of saliva with which the birds glue the dung together are boiled in chicken broth or coconut milk. they are prized as particularly healthful and reputedly strengthen the immune system. in hong kong a kilogram of these strands costs two thousand us dollars.

on the north side of the island there is the so-called viking cave with ancient wall paintings, the origin of which still puzzles scholars. elephants, sailboats, and junks are clearly depicted in rich detail, but it is unlikely that these paintings, as tradition maintains, were actually done by white men from the north.

these days tourists are forbidden to enter the caves. on the other hand, so many excursion boats and snorkelers crowd the maya bay that by now in its natural state this place – where the movie the beach was filmed – looks as artificial as a movie set. as soon as the movie actors left and the public surged in, it was all over with the idyllic paradise. despite the many visitors, the island's red cliffs, deeply carved bays, and coral reefs radiate a special magic. for phi phi leh legal protection came just in the nick of time. for phi phi don it came too late.

the island had long since become pure tourist hype. the government enacted a construction ban and planned to buy back a part of the land from the hotel owners in order to maintain a so-called natural corridor in at least one spot between the two bays. but the growing party culture of phi phi island didn't want the government on the mainland telling them what to do. people didn't need a government on phi phi don. life here evolved according to its own dynamic. the construction ban was simply ignored. the barracks along the usable water reservoirs were filled with workers from the north of thailand. all signs pointed to commercial expansion.

the strict environmental protection restrictions were, however, observed. they even found wide support. the reefs of phi phi island were among the most beautiful in the world. the coral gardens reached as deep as twenty-five meters below sea level and provided habitats for some thousands of species, including leopard sharks, manta rays, and tuna. the diving instructors of phi phi island made the protection of this brilliantly colored submarine world a point of honor. and this protection succeeded. the destruction of the reefs by the anchors of careless recreational sailors stopped. but then nature destroyed them.

since the tsunami of december 26, 2004, an army of volunteer diving teams from all over the world has been busy clearing the coral reefs of the rubble that the second wave deposited. more than three hundred tons of debris, from bits of metal to whole house roofs, have been hauled piece by piece from the sea with bare hands and so-called lifting bags. as they worked, divers kept discovering human remains.

volunteer diving teams were coordinated by andrew hewett and his phi phi recovery dive camp, which devotes itself with painstaking care to collecting broken corals whose polyps have survived and reassembling them in latticed layers.

in this way they are building an artificial reef that will eventually fuse with the natural one. a year after the tsunami i photographed a sign that had been put up on a mangrove tree near the cabana hotel. it said return to paradise. in front of it, at least forty empty beach chairs were set up in military formation. the cabana hotel hadn't yet reopened. in the meantime, the illustration showed bathing towels and tubes of sunblock laid out on the beach chairs. the hotel, whose ground floor had been completely devastated, would eventually resume its idyllic life.

3

in the beginning of august, 2004, when edith and i started to plan a christmas vacation in the south, we actually wanted to go back to jamaica, which we had visited twice. our children, sophie and elias, would be in their last year of school. who knows, we thought, maybe this is our final chance for a vacation together, because next year they won't be living at home anymore, or may have lost interest in family vacations and prefer to go away with their friends. this christmas vacation was supposed to be a sort of early graduation present, or at the very least, a pleasant rest-stop on the way to graduation. i was just about to book another resort in jamaica when we were invited to dinner at sophie's friend dominika's house, and our plans changed.

dominika had been in thailand, on phi phi island, for two weeks in february with her sister and their parents. the first week, dominika's mother said, they stayed in an expensive hotel, the second week, in a hut on a lonely beach. she raved about both weeks. first a week of luxury, then a week in nature. they had booked only their first week from austria. on phi phi island they had then just taken a boat down the coast as far as a secluded bay, and by chance found a hut vacant. the hippie who owned the huts had spoiled them every day with a magnificent breakfast. for days he lay around and played with his three-year-old daughter, at night he lit a fire, grilled fish, and smoked his weed. the first week was lovely, but the second was really terrific. dominika's mother had a lighter printed with the address of this hippie resort, as she called it. she gave me the lighter.

the next day, the woman with whom i had booked many trips said that, if we wanted to go to koh phi phi, we should hurry and make the reservations. christmas is high season, and on phi phi island accommodations can be scarce. just to be sure, i took a brochure about jamaica home with me. but when it turned out that the trip to thailand was substantially cheaper than the one to jamaica, the matter was decided. we booked the phi phi princess, the best bungalow resort this brochure had to offer. i wanted to book both weeks at the same time. elias had other ideas. he didn't want to spend both weeks in a luxury hotel. for the second week, if possible, he wanted to stay in a simple hut like dominika. we let ourselves be overruled and booked a single week in the phi phi princess.

in the following months i wrote several emails to the address on the lighter, without receiving an answer. meanwhile, i began to use the lighter for its actual purpose. after two months, when i still hadn't gotten any reply from the hippie resort, i decided to send a letter. but that wasn't possible anymore. in using the lighter i had worn the address off, and dominika's mother hadn't written it down anywhere either. but she said the resort was easy to find. they had just taken the boat that sailed from the left-hand side of the bay. at first there's a long beach, she told me, then you go around the corner, and soon come to a tranquil little bay. you can only get there by boat. she thought that, with such remote places, even at christmastime, we would find a place to stay. even my brothers, stefan and andreas, said we shouldn't worry unnecessarily about accommodations. everything is really simple there. of course my brothers were still backpackers, and i had given up backpacking quite a while ago.

4

on december 23rd we picked sophie up at the wiedner
gymnasium and then elias at borg 3, an upper-level
realgymnasium in the landstrasse district, to go right to the
airport. on the way our mood changed. edith asked elias what
grade he had gotten in mathematics, and elias had to admit it
was an unsatisfactory. he had promised us up and down that
he was really going to study this time. for months a tutor had
come once a week.
edith said that he'd have to do math every day in thailand.
elias protested. edith said, you're messing up our christmas
vacation, and elias said he didn't care about school, and it went
on like that until elias disappeared when we were already sitting
at the departure gate. sophie went to look for him. after a while
she brought him back. he had just gone to the men's room. we
decided to declare the topic of school taboo for the next two
weeks. but the math textbook still traveled to thailand with us.
we landed in bangkok early on the morning of december
24th. we had to take a bus to another terminal. it took a while
for us to find out where to catch this bus. on the way there we
met a family that looked a bit lost and complained in
unmistakable viennese accents that you couldn't get any
information around here. they were flying on to phuket too.
overtired smokers stood in front of the domestic arrivals
terminal in the warm morning air, which stank of gasoline. for
the most part, they were austrian and german kids. a few of
them indulged in their first thai beer. or maybe they were
continuing a pursuit they had started on the plane.
at phuket airport we waited a long time for our bags, but
we took it in stride. after all, it wasn't the first time we had
waited for luggage in vain. it meant that we had to go to a
special window and identify our bags there from sample
pictures. it also unfortunately meant remembering what had

been packed in which suitcase, which was impossible to do in detail. somehow or other we were supposed to pull together a list. the family from vienna whom we had directed to the inland arrivals terminal in bangkok also stood among those who watched as a suitcase and two bags came around again and again, with nobody picking them up. the man from vienna said these bags probably belonged wherever our baggage was going around and around in some other stupid circle.

when it seemed hopeless that our bags would arrive, we turned to an airport employee. he sent us to a different baggage claim area, and there stood our luggage, neatly lined up against the wall. it had been delivered on the wrong carousel.

a minibus with a driver and a tour guide waited for us in the parking lot. we were the only passengers. on the way we chatted with the tour guide. she said white people all look alike. it was hard for her to tell them apart.

there were still four hours before our ship departed for koh phi phi. the bus took us to a travel agency, in front of which there was a terrace with a table and chairs. we flopped down there, right on a busy street. mostly mopeds passed by, with as many as four people sitting on each. many had sidecars with seats on which four more people could sit.

the toilet was in a closet behind the travel agency. to get there you first had to take your shoes off in the travel agency. but the closet was so filthy that it was wise to take your shoes with you and put them on again there. waiting was so wearisome that we decided to take a walk.

no sooner had we gotten up than a little taxi with an open platform stood beside us. it was basically a converted delivery van with a sawed-off roof. we said no thanks politely, but the driver was adamant. he drove alongside us slowly and every second kept asking us where we were going. the answer that we were just strolling around didn't satisfy him. so i finally asked him whether there was a market nearby. with that, he had us. every few minutes he offered us a further price reduction, until we finally got in because the fare was so ridiculously low.

he dropped us off at a nearby market with jewelry, souvenir, and textile shops, which, we quickly realized, was intended for tourists. the real native market lay behind it. as we walked toward that one, the taxi driver suddenly appeared beside us again, asking what we planned to do. drink something, we said, and the taxi driver offered to take us to a restaurant. we declined, which didn't stop him from continuing to drive beside us. we arrived at a restaurant with a terrace. as we were just about to sit down, the taxi driver jumped out of his car and said we shouldn't go in here because it was a muslim restaurant and they didn't serve alcohol. he would take us to a better restaurant. we begged him to leave us in peace. he got into his car. we stayed there indicating that he should drive away, until he finally did so. then we didn't go into the muslim restaurant anyway because there were only men inside. instead, we sat down at a food stall in the native market in a shack made of wood and corrugated tin where the family that owned it also lived. we bought canned drinks.

i consulted my map for the way back. the road was just sand, with one little market garden after another along it. the plants standing near the entrance were covered with a thick layer of dust. aside from us, there were just a couple of moped drivers and stray dogs in the midday heat. my t-shirt stuck to my body, and i began to long for the taxi driver. when we reached the paved street that led back to our travel agency, we passed a large appliance store with a sign on the door that said air-conditioned. we spent a quarter of an hour pretending to be interested in refrigerators, toasters, and television sets.

in the meantime, a man about sixty years old with thinning hair, with a slender woman who might have been his daughter, had taken seats on the terrace of the travel office. they spoke french. when they weren't talking to each other, the woman read a book, and the man thumbed through a michelin guide to thailand. he wore a gold chain around his neck and had a rolex on his wrist. the woman seemed quite self-confident. she wore a long skirt and a conspicuously large sun hat. then the man left. while i played travel chess with elias, edith struck up a conversation with the woman. she was called emine and came from french switzerland. she put the book aside. it was a diet book. the man came back, and the question, daughter or girlfriend, was soon cleared up. he had brought a bowl of pineapple pieces and gave emine a kiss. later he left again, to get drinks and a noodle dish.

we chatted with him too. his name was claude. like us, they were on their way to koh phi phi. it turned out that they also happened to be staying at the phi phi princess. they had a lot of luggage, including two large suitcases. that reassured us. before leaving, we had wondered whether we should use backpacks for a change, because four suitcases could be really cumbersome on a boat trip. but each of us had assembled so much gear that backpacks were unthinkable.

a minivan took us from the travel office to the harbor. the street went past an endless row of tin-roofed huts, behind which lay a drainage canal covered with primitive wooden planks. you could smell it even from the bus. the harbor pulsed with the intense activity of high season. the ships at dock were crowded so thickly that four or five were tied up together at every pier. in order to reach our ferry we had to cross over three ships. emine and claude found places on the top deck. we went down into the air-conditioned passenger salon. doors on the right and left led to the forward deck, which was populated mostly with young people who sat by their backpacks or lay in the sun.

no sooner had the ship cast off than the people in the comfortable chairs in the passenger salon started to fall asleep, and elias and sophie did too. i went up on deck with my video camera. through the window i filmed elias's head leaning against the window with his mp3 headphones still on. he was used to falling asleep with music in his ears, and his deepest sleep came from the rocking motion of a boat. when he was a little child he once slept in the engine room of a ship. the loud hammering of the diesel generators didn't bother him.

the first islands came into view on the horizon, and we went up on deck. edith and sophie sat in the bow and dangled their feet over the edge. elias followed them later. i filmed them, and then swung around to get the other passengers too. i went inside again and filmed the passengers there. a corpulent man with brown skin had fallen asleep in his chair. i zoomed in on him and captured his face in close-up for a few seconds. i don't know what moved me to film this motionless sleeping face at such length. he was apparently traveling alone, because the seats beside him were still free.

the ship made good headway. when the bow splashed against a wave, it sent up spray. that made a pleasant cool-down in the heat. i just had to be careful not to get the camera wet. beside me at the railing stood a young couple in their twenties who spoke with an english intonation about another couple that had not come along. the woman had long, strangely knotted hair. i filmed her as surreptitiously as possible with a pan to both islands, which were now clearly visible. the closer we came to these islands, the more animated the mood on board became. the kids pulled their digital cameras out of their backpacks, stood up, and photographed. both islands, phi phi don and phi phi leh, burst into view, towering out of the sea. from the distance, phi phi leh, the uninhabited island, looked like a gigantic rock crown, its jagged points covered at the tips with velvety green.

when we had left the seagull-encircled cliffs of phi phi leh behind and approached phi phi don's nearly semicircular ton sai bay, the ship slowed down. it approached another, smaller ship, which was then lashed to our starboard side. some passengers changed boats. among them was a woman with a lot of plastic bags with little gift-wrapped packages peeking out of them. that boat was headed for an island farther out, with which there was no direct connection by ship.

there was a lot of activity in the ton sai bay. the water was crowded with little boats. most were so-called long-tail boats, which functioned as taxis. with their upward-curving prows, they looked a little like venetian gondolas.

in their sterns these boats have motors that can swivel; attached to these are extremely long driveshafts with propellers at the ends. this special construction technique permits the long-tail boats to ride right up onto the beaches. two shovel-shaped boards attached under the keel prevent the boats from tipping over when they are out of the water.

there was no space left for our ship at the concrete jetty on ton sai bay. we passed a barge with large potted plants, which were being watered by a sprinkler system, and we docked in the second row, beside another ferry. the beach was bordered with what seemed like an endless line of long-tail boats moored cheek by jowl. most of the seats were covered with blue canvas, and colorful flower garlands hung on the prows.

a crowd of people awaited us on the pier. some wore uniforms and called out the names of the hotels they represented, others had come with dollies for the luggage. a woman in a blue suit held up a sign with the name phi phi princess. among the new arrivals staying at the phi phi princess, were the four of us, emine and claude, and a family we hadn't met. the woman from the hotel preceded us, and a man pushed the cart with our luggage behind us. diagonally across the way there hung a sign that read welcome to phi phi island.

we walked along a narrow, busy alley, lined with one merchant's stall after another, and before we knew it, we were at the hotel. the reception area of the hotel bordered directly on the market stalls. the numerous receptionists wore long, tight skirts of a pinkish color and matching blouses with an embroidered floral pattern. in the middle of the reception hall, which was open on four sides, stood a rectangular multi-tiered fountain. at the very top there was a large vase with water flowing out over it. the floor was paved with bright tiles. like the entire hall, with its narrow columns, the furniture was made of dark wood. we were served mango drinks to welcome us. the young, attractive receptionist, who showed us to the bungalows, recommended that we reserve a table for christmas dinner. we got drinks vouchers for this too. at five o'clock, she informed us, there would be a champagne reception at the pool, which we should definitely not miss. we still had about an hour and a half to wait before this.

two days later the reception area of the phi phi princess was a garbage dump strewn with corpses. after the catastrophe the hotel website published a list of the employees who died in the tsunami. with photos. there was one of our attractive receptionist among them. forty employees died in the phi phi princess. they left twenty-four orphans behind. the list of the dead employees was later removed from the website, and only the list of the hotel guests from the 26th of december remained on the internet.

5

at first glance the hotel complex of the phi phi princess was a labyrinth overgrown with tall palms and other tropical plants. we couldn't get our bearings right away. aerial views showed no houses, just a forest of palm trees. there were four restaurants and several types of bungalows. the basic category resembled row houses. the middle category included front gardens, where plants proliferated so luxuriantly that you couldn't see the terrace from the path in front. we had rented two bungalows of this category right next to each other. beyond these were the luxury bungalows built right on lohdalum bay. the particularly splendid phi phi princess royal suite was one of these.

two colorful chairs stood on our terrace. they were inspired by gerrit thomas rietveld's red and blue chairs, which i had seen a long time ago as a schoolboy in the then newly-opened viennese museum of the twentieth century. their simple construction, which invited anyone with a rudimentary knowledge of carpentry to copy it, fascinated me. the chairs were made of nothing more than ten slats each, plus two narrow and two wide boards. the narrow boards functioned as arm rests, the wide boards as seats and chair backs. the slats formed the supporting structure of the whole thing. looking at the copies on our terrace, it seemed to me that the chair backs sloped more steeply than in the original, so that they functioned more as a chaise longue than as easy chairs. later i noticed that every terrace had different chairs, all of them copied from classic modern furniture.

at the base of the stairs to each terrace there were basins embedded in the ground so you could wash your feet. our two bungalows were positioned at an angle to each other. when our children were on the terrace we could see them, which may not have seemed like an advantage to them, but which, a day and a half later, turned out to be a little piece of the jigsaw puzzle that helped us survive.

we did what everybody does who checks into a hotel – took a look around, turned off the air-conditioning, which had brought the room temperature down to refrigerator level, and opened the drapes and sliding glass doors. we didn't have a view of the ocean, but in front of us lay a wildly overgrown terrace. nobody could look into our room; here i would have peace and quiet to work. behind the living room was an amazingly huge bathroom, half of which was a shower area, which could be separated from the rest by a curtain.

as we were looking around, beginning to take stock and put our things away, elias discovered a wall safe in the bungalow next door. he put his wallet inside and closed it without first programming a new combination into it. from then on, he didn't have any of his own money.

our first walk was to the beach. the lohdalum bay lay about a hundred meters behind our bungalows. there was no direct way to get to it, only curving, plant-bordered paths that snaked their way through the compound. it was low tide. before us lay a broad, extremely flat beach of fine white sand. the ocean had retreated far out. several boats were beached. we had to wade out to swim. the turquoise water hardly seemed to get any deeper. as beautiful as this beach was, thickly overgrown with palm trees, it didn't exactly seem ideal for swimming. because all four of us like to swim we were going to have to watch the tides and wait for high tide. once we got out far enough we fooled around in the water the way we have always done with our children. in our family water play has something almost ritualistic about it. in the coming days we were certainly going to explore the scuba diving opportunities. there was a bag in the bungalow with our fins, snorkels, and diving masks. two years earlier, during a vacation in jamaica, we had passed the padi diving course for scuba divers.

we discussed everything we wanted to do in the next two weeks, and i tried to reserve my writing and reading time in the bungalow for this vacation, even though experience had taught me that on vacation i often neither wrote nor read but rather smoked, drank, and watched television. as we were leaving the water, the buffets and table for the gala dinner were being set up and decorated on the beach. we met on our terrace for a first glass of champagne. edith appeared in a short black sequined dress and silver sandals. sophie wore a jeans skirt with a white top and a short vest over it, and as for elias, his long, blonde hair – as long and as blonde as my own thirty years ago – hung down over his pale gray blazer. i speak about this with such detail because today none of us owns these clothes, which then seemed like the perfect attire for our christmas party under the palm trees.

since the birth of our twins, it's been my ambition to celebrate christmas as a special family holiday, without the conflicts that often arose during preparations in both my family and edith's. we usually decorated the christmas tree the evening before, and kept it in a closed room during the next day and night. and we would prepare a particularly good, elaborate dinner. it was, like our water games, a shared ritual. we don't take it completely seriously. we play at it.

before exchanging presents we went to a reception at the pool. the swimming pool at the phi phi princess had an unusual location. it was raised on a three meter high base. from up there one had a great view of the bay. on the ocean side the pool ended in a wide waterfall. if one lay on the sand, the ocean was in front and the waterfall behind. if one lay in the pool, the pool water seemed to spill into the wide horizon of the ocean. for the reception, bar tables with a variety of thai snacks had been set up on the pool deck. the waiters served champagne as well as shrimp kebabs and other warm hors d'oeuvres.

most of the two hundred and twenty-one hotel guests came from great britain; the second largest group was from germany; after that came south africa, sweden, canada, the usa, and france. but many other nations were represented: chileans, croats, czechs, danes, dutch, irish, israelis, italians, japanese, mexicans, norwegians, russians, swiss, two thais, and a turk. aside from us, only magdalena and her friend were from austria.

all the guests were dressed up for the reception at the pool. they walked around with their champagne glasses and kebabs and chatted with each other. where do you come from? is this your first thailand vacation? etc. we also met claude and emine again. i took a couple of pictures of this somewhat unreal collection of people who strolled around the pool that evening high above the beach and asked strangers to take pictures of them. even sophie took their pictures. we never saw any of these photographs. two days later roughly half of the people in them were no longer alive.

before we left vienna edith had secretly baked vanilla crescents, which she served us on our terrace after the swimming pool reception. of course, she said, we all agreed that this year the trip would be our christmas present, but if anybody just happened to have brought presents along, then this would be the time to exchange them. we had all brought presents. then we were locked out on the terrace for a while until a bell rang. edith hadn't forgotten the little christmas bell with which, since our children were young, we would ring in our gift-giving ritual. the glass door slid open. the room was lit by candles stuck in silver stars. the christmas presents lay on the chest of drawers and on the double bed. in front of this stood a little plastic christmas tree, which flickered on and off and gradually changed colors until it began to blink again. for a while we watched the strange activity of this kitschy little tree, which seemed to invite the singing of oh tannenbaum. elias took a video of us, but we were laughing at ourselves so hard that we didn't get past the first verse. edith produced a roll of paper with the christmas gospel. sophie read it aloud, and we sang the first verse of silent night. this time we didn't laugh.

then came my christmas speech. this too was a tradition of ours. it included a brief review of the past year and a look ahead. the children would get their diplomas, they would reach majority and have to decide what they wanted to do after graduation. edith and i were about to enter our fifties. and of course i spoke about how lucky we all were to still be together.

and then it was time to unwrap the gifts. we marveled at the items that appeared. perfume, silk underwear, a short-wave radio, a gypsy skirt, a bright red nightgown, an mp3 player, swimming trunks, envelopes with money from opa, oma, and aunt anni, earrings, several USB drives, a chess board. because edith often complained that we could only look at our photos on a computer, sophie had made prints of the best photos of the year.

two presents were promptly tried on. elias gave sophie a t-shirt that read reggae, painted with the colors of the jamaican flag, and along with it a cd he had burned for her with reggae songs by jimmy cliff, desmond dekker, bob marley, peter tosh, seeed, and the gentlemen. for elias sophie had designed a long dark green t-shirt that said ramones in red letters above a black and white picture of the band. the cloth was decorated with metal rivets.

none of these gifts exists anymore, with the exception of the chess board that i got from my children for the apartment in leipzig. because the board is somewhat large, edith persuaded the children to leave it in vienna and just bring a picture of it, which they had cut out of the back of the carton. on the back of this carton, elias wrote that he was looking forward to playing chess with me in leipzig. we unpacked, tried things on, hugged each other, photographed and filmed each other. after our christmas party i locked the video camera in the safe, and that is the reason why i still have it today. two months later it was sent to us from thailand along with the decayed remnants of the rest of the contents of the safe.

6

now, a year and a half later, having written down the memory of our christmas eve, the thought occurs to me to take the camera out of the box, break it open, and see whether the digital tape still contains any accessible information. it's a good time for it, because sophie has just borrowed a digital videocamera from a girlfriend, and this would be an opportunity to play the cassette, in case it still works.

since no part of my camera moves anymore, i pry the cassette holder out with a screwdriver. the cassette is covered with a brown crust. the reels won't turn anymore. i have to break them open too. fine sand trickles out. but the strip of film is wound on both sides, so i get to work. i brush the sand out and then allow half a day to clean the film centimeter by centimeter. then i unspool a length of film from a new cassette, cut it, and glue the thailand film to the ends of this unused film. to be sure that i don't lose what i'm about to see, i connect the videocamera to the computer and simultaneously start making a copy.

the film begins with a raucous st. nicholas day party in our apartment in vienna, where no nicholas appears, but instead his companion krampus, whom we endearingly call luzi (for lucifer). at times the colors blur a bit, and the sound is somewhat distorted, but in general the film seems to be in working order. and then come the first sequences from the boat trip to koh phi phi. i stare transfixed at the screen. elias asleep, the pans across the people on the forward deck and to the islands. and then the pan in the passengers' salon and the close-up of the corpulent sleeping man. and suddenly i recognize the face again. two days after i took this picture, i had to look at it over and over. his brown skin had already yellowed. he was one of the dead who lay in the entrance area of the hotel in which we had taken refuge. he had a deep open wound in his stomach, from which there trickled a liquid. near him lay a dead woman and child. to this day, i don't know if they belonged with him. maybe he had just taken a trip to phuket or made a business trip and was traveling back to his family on our ship.

the film ends with our christmas party. i see us singing o tannenbaum and laughing. the tree had obviously just switched to red, because we're singing: how red your leaves are. the colors get blurrier, and finally edith sits on the bed unpacking the red silk nightgown that she got from the children. she stands up and slips it on. at this moment the sound begins to crackle, and the colors radiate out beyond their outlines. red squares fly out of edith's body, and there is now a black spot where her face was. the film ends there.

7

a year after the tsunami edith and i return to koh phi phi. i have started writing down what i remember. it turns out that, in many cases, the images in my head are very vague. in particular i have no memory of the circumstances that saved our lives. that's a question that has tormented me all these months. why am i still alive? why are we all still alive? i want to see the place again, or what's left of it. i want to talk to people on koh phi phi. i want to know how the local people are coping.

on a website i read that there is going to be a big memorial service on the first anniversary of the tsunami in ton sai village. but i have no desire to spend christmas on phi phi island again, and certainly not without the children.

under no circumstances do they want to come along. nor is edith attracted to thailand. and so it seems best that i should travel at the beginning of december in order to be home for christmas. but edith doesn't want to let me travel alone. she decides to come with me. because it is cheaper, and because i have business there, i book us a flight from munich.

there's a problem during check-in an hour and a half before our flight in early december. the lufthansa employee can't access the flight data in the computer. she tries to telephone, but the line is busy. she tries it again via computer and shakes her head. for some reason flight 925 of thai airways international has not been given clearance. meanwhile there's a change of shift, but the next employee cannot solve the problem and suggests that we try again in a quarter-of-an-hour. when we finally return to the counter we find an overly friendly employee. she turns the screen around to us and lets us choose our own seats. she points to row 31. seats a, b, and c have extra leg room. but she doesn't have access to those, they are only assigned at the gate. that's where we should ask for these seats. in the meantime she's going to give us two seats next to which there's a third one free.

at the gate i ask about row 31, seats a through c. taken, says the employee. i'm satisfied with this answer and take it to be confirmation that when it comes to seat choice, privileges are principally given to other people. i can still hear the man standing next to me giving his bad back as the reason for

needing a certain seat near the emergency exit.
later when the flight is announced, it's not done by
separate seating classes, but all at once. we give ourselves time
until most of the people have disappeared onto the walkway to
the plane. then there's an announcement. edith and i are
requested to come to the gate. the employee tells us that now
we can have seats 31 a through c. i don't know how it
happened and i don't ask any questions. i just say thank you. in
a boeing 707 row 31 seats a, b, and c are the first three seats by
the door in economy class. opposite us a thai stewardess takes
her seat for take-off. she smiles at us and says we have the best
seats. she points to the bulge in the door where the emergency
chute is obviously stored. after take-off she says, i'm allowed to
put my feet up there. i thought of this myself but was sure that
this additional privilege wouldn't last long.

edith takes a little package out of her backpack. it's a
present from her friend claudia. it came with instructions to
open it in the airplane. in the small container, which looks like
a miniature hatbox, there's a little gold chain with a guardian
angel.

when she puts the chain on, i am overcome by a strange
sense of panic. suddenly i'm afraid that i'm making a huge
mistake. i could have been satisfied and happy that all four of
us survived. instead i'm exposing us to new danger. a tsunami
can come again at any time, and an airplane can always crash.
who knows why the aircraft wasn't cleared shortly before take-
off? maybe it has mechanical problems. am i going to make the
children into orphans because i'm too stubborn to appreciate a
fortunate escape from danger?

i don't give voice to my thoughts, but they torment me for
hours and it would be nice to know if edith shares the same
fears. we don't talk about it; i don't want to upset her.

the plane to bangkok is filled with men who want to enjoy
this short life as much as possible. most of them travel in
groups. they want to start having fun in the airplane, and here
that's not difficult. thai airlines has plenty of alcohol on board.

behind us sits a german with his thai wife. as we boarded the airplane, he had suggested that we switch rows.

the individual men or those traveling in groups stay over in bangkok or continue on to pattaya; the couples gather in front of the gates to other destinations at the seaside. in the departure terminal of the bangkok airport there are many rows of seating made of steel tubes covered in blue leatherette. the floor is carpeted in a pattern of bright checks. the ceiling is an uninterrupted network of fluorescent lighting strips in a grate pattern. here and there television consoles are mounted on stands.

we recognize this terminal. cnn is still playing on the tv sets. back then all they showed were pictures of the tsunami. today it's mostly pictures of the trial of saddam hussein. along the row of gates where the airport employees are now tearing tickets and feeding them into automatic readers, there stood tables with the delegates of different embassies. at one end of the terminal they had apparently removed some of the rows of steel seating to make room for a first aid station. at the other end there are the toilets, as there were then, and the smoking area, which is separated from the rest of the hall by a glass wall. the glass is decorated with flower-patterned stickers. two horizontal bars have been left clear, through which you can see how many smokers are sitting on the hard blue molded plastic chairs.

a year ago i sat on one of those chairs. a lufthansa stewardess sat down opposite me and gave me a cigarette. she promised she would get us some socks. edith was afraid of spending eleven hours barefoot in an air-conditioned cabin. we didn't have any shoes, only plastic sandals. a couple of hours after the tsunami a man had found a sealed bag filled with flip-flops in the garbage dump of a destroyed sporting goods store. he had helped himself and brought the rest up to the roof where we, along with fifty other people, had found our new quarters on phi phi island.

on the evening of december 28, 2004, when we were

sitting in this departure terminal of the bangkok airport, it was still unclear whether we were going to be able to take off. austrian airlines had refused to take us to vienna because we had booked our thailand flight with a different airline. lufthansa took us to munich, and eva, to amsterdam, but austrian air wouldn't pick up the last leg of the trip from munich or amsterdam to vienna. for two days after the tsunami austrian airlines flew back to vienna with empty seats. they wouldn't accept passengers without austrian air tickets.

the night flight of december 28 from bangkok to vienna was the turning point. after many telephone calls from the embassy employee in charge of our case, austrian air complied and filled its planes with people who had no tickets or weren't able to buy any because they had lost everything. because it took a while until departure at 11:00 p. m. and our wounds had already been dressed at the first aid station, i began to focus on small things like socks. austrian air could or would not be helpful, but the lufthansa stewardess who had promised me socks gave some to us. in our condition, with bandages and dressings all over our bodies, she made us very happy.

just before departure, when we had already moved to the gate, our trip home became uncertain again. two children who had lost their parents had been brought to the airport. it turned out that there was just room for them in the airplane.

austrian airlines loosened its protocol two days later and even sent special planes to phuket to bring stranded passengers home.

8

our 2004 vacation began with christmas day on phi phi island. our impression of what the island was like before the tsunami came from walking around on this one day.

there were no motor vehicles. they wouldn't have had any room in the narrow, bustling alleys. if one wanted to get to distant points on the island one had to take a boat or equip oneself to walk along one of the simple jungle paths that go over the mountains.

our christmas day began with an elaborate breakfast in the octagonal dining pavilion located directly on the beach. next to it were the steps that led up to the pool. you could sit under the high pointed roof of the pavilion, visible from all around, or out on the beach where more tables with sun umbrellas were set up among the hibiscus, oleander, and azalea bushes, and the palm trees. under the pool terrace there was a bar, built into the base of the pool, facing the beach, right next to the waterfall. directly above this bar there was a second, round one, to serve swimmers who could sit on barstools in the water. we had seen the pool at the christmas reception. on the last day we could use it, but as it turned out, we had no need for it. there was another building attached to the back of this enormous pool base. this structure included the kitchen on its ground floor. above this was the hotel spa area, which one could reach by climbing up a few steps from the pool terrace.

as i return a year later, i see this building compound with different eyes. the spa area is where magdalena and her boyfriend survived. they had stopped at the pool terrace and taken a lot of pictures of the wave as it approached them. magdalena later emailed me these photos, which is why i can understand why there was amazement at first, but not the least bit of panic. the wave looked harmless.

the people at the pool stared out to sea because the water had retreated so very far out at high tide. it was barely visible on the horizon. the motor boats anchored at some distance from the beach, which even at low tide always had water under their keels, had tipped over and now lay directly on the ocean floor. beyond them, the coral reefs were completely exposed. people were astonished at this strange drama, so they photographed it. after a few minutes you could see the ocean returning in the distance. it looked like a silver band on the horizon, and it approached very quickly – in any case, noticeably faster than a normal ocean wave. since then the speed of this wave has been calculated. it had raced through the andaman ocean at 320 km. per hour and slowed to 50 km. per hour on the flat ocean floor at phi phi island. behind it, however, there the water surged at the original, faster, speed. as a result the flat wave, initially almost 100 km in length, became shorter and shorter and became compressed into a growing mountain of water. what the people at the pool saw was just the forerunner of that wave, a kind of whitewater rapids that ploughed up the sandy bottom of the bay.

this brown, sediment-filled band of foam grew as it rolled into lohdalum bay, reaching a length of about 200 meters. but its front edge – the portion directly approaching the beach – was barely two meters high. seen from the distance it did not look threatening. what the people on the pool deck couldn't immediately make out – because you could hardly distinguish it from the normal view of the ocean's horizon – was the slanted forward edge of the wall of water surging right behind it. the water level kept rising until it reached a height of 6 meters above normal high tide. three vacationers ran to their motorboats. the wave pushed some water toward the shore, which lifted the boats. the three vcationers started their motors and sped at full throttle into the wave. two of the boats made it to the crest; the other was yanked over and engulfed by the mass of water. the people at the pool gasped, not because of the wave, but because of the man at the helm. nothing more was seen of him or the boat. that was when the swimmers on the beach realized the danger and began to run. one of the two other boats, which seemed to have crested the wave, capsized immediately in the roiling surf. the bow went under and the boat disappeared. up at the pool there did not yet seem to be any danger. people were talking about the boat owner who had possibly just drowned before their very eyes and keeping an eye on what was going to happen next.

at this point the acting general manager of the phi phi

princess, supansa yodaroon, was sitting at breakfast discussing the gala dinner for new year's eve with the accountant and the purchasing manager for food and drink. as the ocean withdrew they stood up and walked a few steps out in front of the pavilion. they looked out onto the bay until the water returned. then they saw the boats capsizing and ran up to the pool.

the wave hit the beach and swept everything along with it; beach chairs, umbrellas, beach towels, seats. water came up onto the shore and flowed past the pool. it grabbed the tables, chairs, and bushes from the dining pavilion, washed them into the restaurant, and spat them out the other side.

the sea had become a broad flood that flowed out across the land and kept rising until it was obvious that it would soon reach the height of the pool. then the people up there began to run – some were too late. they were swept into the pool, where a vortex formed and pushed them under. others ran up the few steps to the fitness center or tried to climb onto the roof. the flood kept rising with increasing speed.

behind the spa area there were two terraces, one adjacent to the fitness center. magdalena's boyfriend managed to run out in time and avoid the direct line of the current, but magdalena hesitated too long. she was swept through the fitness center and flung against the wall, where she broke her ankle. the seawater now flowed through the fitness center over the terrace. magdalena and her friend hung onto the handrails. they watched as bungalows were swept away and people tried to climb up palm trees and onto roofs.

the three resort managers who had gathered to discuss the new year's buffet were standing on this terrace. before their eyes the wave crashed through the palm trees and splintered everything not made of solid concrete. the exquisite bungalows collapsed like matchboxes. the managers had no idea of the drama taking place behind them in the kitchen area.

bustling activity was in progress there and in the contiguous pantries and supply rooms. some employees were clearing away the breakfast buffet and washing dishes. others were preparing the noonday buffet, which was supposed to begin in an hour and a half. the kitchen entrance was on the dining pavilion side. when the wave hit, it barricaded the door with debris, tables, and storage cupboards. to escape, the employees would have had to shove the barricade away against the current, which was impossible. the kitchen area was soon completely submerged.

9

on christmas morning when we sat down in this octagonal dining pavilion with its clear view of the ocean, we were pleased with the rich variety of fresh fruit. two cooks stood nearby, ready to make omelets. we watched the people, met emine and claude, and – as we discovered nine months later – were ourselves being watched by magdalena and her boy friend, who sat at the table next to us and recognized us as austrians by our accents.

the previous evening, after our christmas dinner edith and i had taken a walk on the beach promenade on the arbor side of ton sai bay. our children, who had barely slept during the flight, watching plenty of movies instead, were too tired to join us. at breakfast we told them about the many bars and discos we had passed, and about the wild partying and the fire shows.

we saw people swinging ropes of fire – the so-called fire-jugglers – at the beach bars. there was a real contest going on to see who could paint the most artistic fire figures in the night. one juggler in particular caught our attention because he was still a child, maybe eight years old. inspired by the not-quite-sober kids watching him, he moved to a techno rhythm, surrounding himself with fiery ribbons so intricately woven that they challenged the masters of this traditional art. one man in the audience was conspicuous, a tall german dressed in boots and tanga shorts, showing off his tattoos.

we watched this raucous activity – so different from

anything we were used to seeing at christmastime – for a while, then bought a bottle of red wine and went back to our bungalow to have a glass on our terrace. at breakfast, when we told the children about our expedition into the local nightlife, it became pretty clear what they would be doing that evening.

but first we got our swimming things from the bungalows and went in search of a fairly quiet place. we walked along lohdalum bay past the last hotel, the phi phi viewpoint resorts, and continued uphill for a bit to view the bungalows and their location. after all it was plausible that in the second week of our vacation we might rent here. a day later at approximately the same time magdalena would be carrried by her boyfriend up this same stretch of the mountain, followed by many others seeking safety from new waves.

this path climbed steeply upwards, with a fork that led to the viewpoint, a lookout platform with a view over both bays. when the tsunami arrived there were a few tourists at the viewpoint. they photographed and videotaped continuously without really understanding what they were filming. the chronicle of their snapshots later brought some clarity to the debate about when and where the water came. in one of these pictures, later put on the internet, you can see the ships in ton sai bay racing away at top speed. the passenger ferry from phuket is among them. she had docked at the pier at ten o'clock. like us the day before, the vacationers and day-tourists were greeted by the sign saying welcome to phi phi island. it still hung there after the tsunami. the vacationers went to their hotels. the day-tourists strolled through the byways of ton sai village or sat down at one of the cafés on the beach promenade. when the passenger ship had been docked at the pier for a quarter of an hour, it suddenly plunged down like a freight elevator. the lines strained and pulled the ship tighter against the wooden planks that acted as bumpers along the concrete pilings sunk into the earth, but it kept on sinking until the stern lay in the sand. that had never happened before. the gangplank, which normally sloped from the ship down to the concrete platform of the pier, now hung upside-down so steeply that it slid backwards onto the deck.

the sea came back fast. as soon as he had water under his keel, the captain of the passenger ship did the only right thing: he cast off and headed into the wave at full speed. the picture of ton sai bay taken from the viewpoint shows a boat race. approximately thirty larger and smaller motor boats are drawing long white lines in the blue water. the ones that took part in this race escaped. the wave from ton sai bay had several levels that only reached a total height of about three meters above normal high tide, but that was enough to hurl those boats moored at the shoreline far up onto land and smash them against buildings. a moment later everything left of them was washed back into ton sai bay by the much higher and more powerful wave that came from lohdalum bay. in the end, the sea in ton sai bay was a carpet of floating debris.

on our christmas day walk, we found the bungalows of the phi phi viewpoint resorts. all were constructed in the same style, with decks built on posts over the hillside offering their occupants beautiful ocean views. but these weren't the simple huts we wanted for our second vacation week, so we turned around and followed the contour of the bay. the terrain of the sandy beach changed into a flat ridge of cliffs. behind them rose a steep mountain overgrown with thick jungle vegetation. the flat stones were broken up by narrow grooves teeming with countless shellfish and crabs that had washed up. as soon as one got near them these animals disappeared beneath the stones.

we stayed here a while and went into the water now and then, pleased that we had only to walk a few minutes beyond the main beach to be all alone. i can't lie quietly in the hot sun, so i walked along the jungle border and stumbled on bits of flotsam caught in the roots of some trees. i found a long rope, stripped a few branches off bushes, and built a sunshade on our cliff ledge from all of this.

on the way back to the hotel we had lunch at an indian food stall. then we went our separate ways. edith and sophie settled down on the beach in the shadow of a broad shade tree. elias went back to the bungalow, and i wanted to have a little look around. a group of gardeners was busy pruning and watering the plants on the paths of our hotel compound. i liked it here so much that, despite our agreement, i went to the hotel reception desk and inquired whether we could spend another week here. the receptionist said their bungalows were already booked, but she would take a closer look when she had time and get back to me with an offer. i glanced into the clothing, jewelry, and souvenir boutiques and then went into the phi phi princess diving shop, the scuba diving concession in our hotel. there i spoke with a man i now know was the swede named per. i found his picture among the photos documented in phi phi island – a paradise lost. per's thai girlfriend, joy, was also sitting in the shop. per had first come to the island eleven years earlier, and returned annually ever since. he got his license as a scuba diving instructor. since then he would spend the cold season on phi phi island and the summer in sweden.

he explained to me that phi phi island offered excellent scuba diving conditions, with an underwater visibility of twenty to thirty meters. his diving groups consisted of a maximum of five people, so our family was the perfect size. because we couldn't produce an up-to-date logbook, he recommended that we begin with a refresher course in the coastal reefs and then the following day at the earliest explore the extensive underwater caves, with manta rays several meters wide. the way he stretched out his arms i imagined such a gigantic fish that i answered i wasn't really sure i wanted to meet one.

joy listened to us and laughed. she was, as i learned later, pregnant, in her fifth month. two days after my encounter with per and joy, the 27th of december, would have been their wedding day.

joy's real name was actually suchada pattakor, but

everybody called her joy. she was twenty-five years old and came from kathu, a town on the island of phuket. per and joy had met two years before. the previous summer per had taken her to sweden and introduced her to his family. they had decided to give up their adventurous life on phi phi island after the birth of their child and move to sweden for good. but that would never be. the next morning per led a small group of divers out to the king cruiser, a shipwreck in twenty-five meters of water half-way to phuket. it had become a favorite scuba diving destination. after about twenty minutes, they broke off their dive because the water became murky and a strong current developed. they were feeling the edge of the wave that was speeding toward lohdalum bay.

joy had been sitting in the phi phi princess diving shop since eight-thirty in the morning. experience showed that most customers came in right after breakfast. there were two british diving instructors with her in the shop. one of them, chay kyme, later described what followed to a reporter for the new york times. they ran to the reception area. water surged into the lobby. they climbed onto the reception desk and watched it flow past. the wave had come from ton sai bay. everybody who still had the chance to run away fled to the other side of the island, to lohdalum bay. but that's where the much bigger wave hit. it crashed over the island, a surging, tearing current, and flattened the reception hall of the phi phi princess. both of the british diving instructors were washed out through one of the alleys over the narrow land bridge into the harbor bay, where they were later pulled up onto a long-tail boat. just like the receptionists, per's girlfriend, joy, was killed when the lobby of the phi phi princess collapsed.

per spent the next weeks being useful, collecting corpses and combing through the garbage dump that the island had become. in doing so, he discovered his fiancée's remains. in the swedish documentary volume, phi phi island – a paradise lost, there is a shot of per. he has his green face mask hanging off one ear. it dangles under his unshaven cheek. he wears a red, sweat-stained baseball cap. the sun is reflected in his bloodshot eyes, and a ring hangs from his silver necklace.

after the tsunami, vacationers like us, who had survived, fled home as fast as they could. it didn't dawn on me until i returned to the island a year later that there had been a countermovement of former phi phi island vacationers from every corner of the globe arriving to help. carlito's, a bar that belonged to the swede carl steiner, who had lived on the island for ten years, became the center that coordinated the operations of these volunteers. the whole interior of the bar had been destroyed by the tsunami, but the building itself survived the wave. the volunteer aid workers from help international – hi phi phi for short – met here every evening. this organization, financed completely by donations, was founded by the dutchman emiel kok, who once had a scuba diving business on phi phi island. when he heard about the destruction of the island, he gave up his work in the netherlands and came back to help.

at its peak, hi phi phi employed sixty-seven thai workers, aided by over two thousand volunteer helpers. the greatest portion of the piles of debris left on the island after the tsunami were not removed by backhoes but by hand. this had the advantage that passports, luggage tags, and other clues to people who had been on the island during the tidal wave weren't thrown away, but were saved to aid in the painstaking work of identifying the missing.

after a few months, when most of the mountains of debris had been removed, the mission of hi phi phi changed. directors of this aid organization believed that tourists shouldn't take work away from locals who had lost everything in the flood. instead, tourists should return as tourists. so hi phi phi was reorganized as a nonprofit to sell handicrafts and t-shirts with the motto return to paradise in its shops. all proceeds went to benefit the reconstruction. the people on phi phi island didn't see much of the many millions in tsunami aid that flowed toward phi phi island. the government compensation for the total loss of a business was around four hundred euros. for the death of a family member, forty euros. the thai government wanted to prevent the reconstruction of ton sai village. it planned to establish a nature park on the narrow strip of land between the two bays with a monument to memorialize the disaster. ton sai village would be relocated up the hill and connected to the harbor by cable car. none of this will ever happen. already more shops and service businesses line the narrow streets than before the destruction. and even the hotels that could claim total loss, like the phi phi princess and the charlie, are doing active, if somewhat restricted, business again. their managements are eager to get reconstruction permits for their properties. the dining pavilion of the phi phi princess is now a beach restaurant. people are again cooking in its kitchen – this death-trap – though only minimally, for day-tourists.

10

a year later, just a few palm trees remain standing between the bar and the beach. everything else left was debris and had to be bulldozed away. a couple of rough footpaths lead across open spaces that are otherwise overgrown with grass and flowers. mopeds now travel in this no man's land. a girl on a kid's bicycle comes along. edith and i get out of the way; the girl laughs in our direction. behind her on the luggage rack sits a small, barefoot boy holding onto her for dear life.

five tents are set up in a row, but unoccupied. behind a wooden shack hangs a shower, with a yellow water hose connecting it to the tappear tattoo bar.

a year after the tsunami i have a need to look up all the places i can remember and walk the paths i walked on that christmas day in 2004. after my visit to phi phi princess diving, i had looked for a different path to ton sai bay and assumed that houses, and therefore also paths, must exist at the foot of the mountain, where the two bays lie farthest apart. so i passed by the tappear tattoo bar. it was a bar like many others, a multistory wooden building in which the owner's family lived and worked. downstairs they cooked and served. upstairs, there were two rented rooms with a terrace. at the very top, right under the roof, there were one or two more private rooms. the building was surrounded by stools, tables, hammocks, and wooden deck chairs with blankets and pillows that let you stretch out as much as you wanted. next door the time & tide bar didn't look much different. both resembled the hippies bar and the rolling stoned bar, which we had passed the evening before. what distinguished the tappear tattoo bar from the others was the fact – considering local conditions, not all that remarkable – that you could get a tattoo here.

since the tsunami, however, the tappear tattoo bar is a true rarity. seen from lohdalum bay it is the first building that withstood the inundation. earlier the bar had been hidden way back in a little rundown alley. the bungalows of the charlie hotel stood in front of it. in front of them there was the promenade with all the little food stands, pizza stands, cafés, and restaurants. now the tattoo bar stands front and center.

it is late morning. a couple sits on barstools drinking cocktails. these two are the only guests. on one wall hangs a picture of the emperor and on the other wall, one of bob marley. there is reggae playing. the barkeeper stands there barechested. he has a baby in his arms, proudly introducing him by holding him out over the bar. it's a boy, he says. he's exactly a hundred days old today.

his two pretty daughters, one maybe thirteen and with braces on her teeth, the other perhaps fifteen, are in the open kitchen busily preparing lunch. i consider quickly and say: then he was probably conceived before the tsunami.

yes, the barkeeper answers, he brought us luck. we all survived.

i tell him that we were staying in the phi phi princess and we, too, all managed to get out.

in the phi phi princess, he says, shaking, his head, in the phi phi princess. then you were really lucky.

i ask: were you here in the bar when the water came?

he begins to tell his story, then interrupts himself to hand the baby over to his wife, who is busy in a room behind the kitchen with another child, perhaps a year and a half old. his daughters stop working and come to the bar. even the couple, who, it soon becomes clear, comes from australia, begin to get interested in the story. the barkeeper tells us that he felt the earthquake in the early morning and went to the ocean several times to check the water. when he saw it retreating suddenly, he took a couple of bottles of water from the refrigerator and went up the mountain with his family.

he pulls big shrink-wrapped photographs out of a drawer. these show the bar the way it was when he came down from the mountain. wedged in a landscape of debris, as far as you can see it's the only building standing. then from the same drawer he takes out a documentary book, phi phi island – a paradise lost. the first part of the book contains pictures of the island as it looked before the tsunami. the second part documents the devastation. i leaf through, but the sight of these photos makes me so nervous that i put the book aside. i absolutely want this book, but i can't look at the pictures. the barkeeper says i can buy it in the hi phi phi store.

in the following days i try hard to get hold of this book, with no luck. it's sold out in the hi phi phi store and both bookshops in ton sai village. everybody i ask knows this book, which originated from the initiative of a swede who loved phi phi island and knew carlito's owner, carl steiner. but it seems to be completely sold out – until i discover it by chance a couple of days later in the adventure-club. the owner, an englishman, sells it to me. the proceeds from this book support the reconstruction work. when i tell the englishman that we were in the phi phi princess and, later, on the roof of the phi phi hotel, he tells his clerk to burn me a cd with the amateur videos and pictures he has collected. some among the film sequences and photos were taken from the roof of the phi phi hotel.

i ask him how he survived.

i was in the shop with my wife and child, he told me. then people suddenly shouted, the water is coming, the water is coming. we ran over to the reggae bar, because it had several floors. we stayed safe there. afterward i made my way back to the store alone. i wanted to see if there was anything left. then the second wave came. i couldn't get back to the bar anymore. so i climbed up onto the roof here and watched the water destroy the whole street.

the englishman slaps his hand against the concrete column of the adventure club. this withstood it, fortunately, he says. the rubbish that lay all around here came from the buildings that had been swept away. everything that belonged to us disappeared. we've had to start over from scratch.

he casts a glance around the shop, as if he could still picture the old set-up. then he puts a strange question to us. he wants to know how much time passed between the first and second waves. was it just five minutes? he asks, or twenty minutes? or was it maybe even longer? he hasn't been able to figure it out yet. no one who lived through it has been able to answer the question for him. we are stumped too. we have often spoken about it with our children, without coming up with an answer.

it seems as if we all lost our sense of time. we had blundered into a world so different that the old way of perceiving time didn't apply. people couldn't grasp what they saw, but, at the same time, they tried to comprehend the image it presented as reality. i think i remember that people wept and shrieked – and the videotapes prove it too. but the picture that first comes to mind when i think about it is of a massive paralysis, a sort of universal stasis. nobody was looking at a watch.

the clerk at the adventure club has finished burning the cd. he brings it to his boss, who hands it to me and requests that i not give these pictures to the press. they're not for profit. as a farewell, he shakes my hand and wishes me good luck.

11

now i had the book and a cd with videos and still photos. i browsed through the book and put it aside again. i viewed a few still pictures on the cd or looked at the shaky videos and turned them off again. i had already made up my mind to write about this, but i wasn't yet ready to look at these pictures. nor did i know that the book i had bought documenting the tsunami included a photo of me. i just noticed that yesterday, a year and a half after the tsunami, when i picked up the book again and went through it page by page. first i came across per, the scuba diving instructor at the phi phi princess who had lost his pregnant fiancée, and then a picture showing an improvised outdoor first aid station – or better put, injured vacationers who have flopped onto mattresses on the beach to wait for their wounds to be bandaged. the picture was taken on december 27th around nine in the morning. the tsunami was the day before. a helicopter had flown in nurses and bandages. before it departed, approximately fifty corpses that had been collected on the beach were stacked into the aircraft. according to islamic rite, they had to be buried immediately.

on the mattress in the foreground of the picture there lies a white man with slashed arms and a bound-up leg. a thai woman is trying to place a pillow under his foot. the man writhes in agony and buries his face in the pillow. emine and i are sitting on another mattress in the center of the picture. during the previous night, emine had become our third child. she has lacerated shins like me, and is still wearing the thick white head bandage that i tore from a bed sheet and put on her the day before. i'm wearing the green t-shirt with the logo of the iowa international writing program. seeing this t-shirt i can remember how it smelled: like oil and sewage. the tsunami had torn open the septic tanks and fuel tanks in the marina. in the picture i am just undoing the bandage on my left hand. emine has also lifted her hands up to her head bandage. she is probably just about to take it off. a thai nurse comes toward us. she wears a head-covering of the sort used in operating rooms. we are about to get our first medical attention. behind us a woman wearing white rubber gloves has sat down, exhausted, in the sand. more injured people wait on other mattresses. a man stands nearby with a cupboard door. such doors were used as stretchers for the injured and the dead. in the background the characteristic cliffs of lohdalum bay tower over this group.

12

in the evening, on our return visit, edith and i go back to the tapear tattoo bar. the music is loud. they're playing reggae there again. there aren't many people. some are lying in hammocks, others have stretched out on the cots that are covered with pillows and blankets. the chairs and benches are free. the bar owner is pleased that we have returned. he shakes our hands. even his daughters shake our hands and laugh. where's the baby? edith asks. it's sleeping with its mother inside, he says, and points to the door behind the kitchen, where he had delivered the baby at noon. or maybe they're watching television, he adds. neither would be that easy given this loud music.

we study the drinks menu. edith orders a piña colada. the thai bartender says sex on the beach is their surprise drink here. i inquire how they mix the cocktail sex on the beach. he says he mixes it according to each individual customer, and i order one. he seems to pour a slug from every bottle into the shaker. then he shakes it to the rhythm of the music with strength and persistence, as if we're going to have his percussion accompaniment to the reggae for the rest of the evening. next to us a swede and an englishman order a bottle of local sang som whiskey and a couple of cans of cola to go with it. one of the owner's two daughters brings a plastic bucket with ice. everything is poured into this and then drunk through a straw. the swede lets me have a taste. the cheapest drink, he says. everyone has it here. the drink is called swedish bucket; it's normally served in a plastic beach bucket with straws. during our walk on christmas eve a year ago i noticed these buckets, but didn't know what people were drinking out of them. the swede tells me that he was here from february to may to help with the clean-up. that's why he gets everything cheaper. (i actually did wonder why he had to pay only 200 baht for the bottle of sang som and both cans of cola). his friend, the englishman, is apparently responsible for the tattoos that are available in this bar as a kind of sideline. he pulls up his t-shirt and shows me his completely tattooed torso. now and then the swede and the englishman play darts. both of the owner's daughters watch them with interest.

a new bartender begins his shift, a white guy with dreadlocks who gives the impression of being completely mellow. now and then he slips into the little room behind the wooden staircase to the second floor to change the music. then he turns the music off and puts a microphone on the floor. he takes a long bamboo reed from the wall, from which, standing like a swiss alpenhorn player, he coaxes deep, pulsing notes. the sound reminds me of a jaw harp. later he explains to me that this roughly two meter long pipe is actually an australian aborigine instrument. he lets me try it. we find out that the dreadlocked guy is from italy. he's been living on phi phi island for ten years. before that he traveled around the world, and here's where he landed. when the tsunami came he was still in bed. he was lucky because he lived in a cheap hut high up the mountainside. when i order a whiskey-cola, the bartender says i should go ahead and order a bottle of sang som and a can of cola, then i'd get more for my money. but i don't want to drink from a sand bucket, i prefer a glass. it's all cool to the dreadlocked guy. next to us an australian kid is having his calf tattooed. two girls are watching while they smoke and take pictures. you look so sexy, one of them keeps saying. the owner's wife comes out of the room behind the kitchen with the baby and disappears upstairs. we say goodnight.

along the path that begins behind the tapear tattoo bar there is a sprawl of cheap shops, simple wooden huts, tents, bars, and snack booths. in the cheapest grocery store that we have come across in a long time, we buy a bottle of gin and a couple of tonics. a man sits at the cash register. near him on cots lie a woman and two children watching television. i notice the long scar on the woman's knee. i look around the room and see brick walls with holes that have been patched with cement. i point to the woman's scar and ask whether that was the tsunami. and then she tells me, not sadly, but laughing. the children keep watching the television. they were trapped in the collapsing house and were just able to escape at the last second. she was later operated on in the hospital in krabi. now she has metal plates in her leg and has to have a second operation. we're lucky, she says, we survived.

she looks at both her children and pats them on the head, but they're so fascinated by the tv they don't even seem to notice their mother's gesture.

at one stand we buy a couple of dvds. we want to go back to our hotel along the path past the reservoir, but the path is so covered with puddles from today's rain that we soon turn around and trust our luck to the newly paved tourist paths.

we come back here the next day. edith is taking this path for the first time. when i discovered it behind the bungalows of the charlie resort on christmas day, she didn't come along. at the beginning of the path behind the tapear tattoo bar there were a lot of small shops even back then. the farther one got from the bay, the more primitive the dwellings became. they were huts of corrugated steel and wooden shacks nailed together. along the path there stood a few rows of simple bungalows with the doors open, where kids were sleeping off their hangovers, their clothes tossed into colorful heaps. laundry was drying on the railings of the wooden steps. then i came to a large water basin guarded by two uniformed men sitting in the shade of a little house and smoking. it was the irrigation reservoir of phi phi island. on the other bank there stretched a compound of barracks.

a year later the irrigation reservoir is a bulldozed mudhole and the barracks have disappeared. they used to house the construction workers from northern thailand. the previous evening they had been celebrating and wanted to sleep it off on the second day. when the tsunami came most of them were still on their cots. they were washed into the irrigation reservoir along with the huts that crashed down around them.

the irrigation reservoir was the most horrible sight you could see after the tsunami on phi phi island: a lake of debris and corpses. approximately sixty dead bodies floated in the water. at first you could hardly tell the corpses from the debris, but within a few hours the bodies swelled up like balloons. in the course of the next weeks, three times as many corpses were fished out of the basin. very few of the construction workers from northern thailand survived.

a year later people stand on the edge of this pit of filth and look into their memories. in place of the barracks there rises the skeleton of a two-story concrete building. nearby a little row of bungalows has been built. closely crowded together, they don't have doors or windows yet. the pump house, where the guards sat and smoked in the shade, has been renovated and freshly painted. no pump or filter mechanisms can be seen through the louvers, just a big pile of cement sacks. a sign indicates that the reconstruction of the irrigation system has been made possible by a tsunami relief grant from the danish government.

three places on phi phi island were the deadliest. one was around this irrigation reservoir; another was practically in the middle of ton sai village, where the two waves met and the higher one rolled over the lower. there the employees of the surrounding hotels, and in some cases their families, lived in a settlement of huts. today it's an open area still piled with debris. the colliding waves smashed the huts to pieces there and shot the corrugated metal and posts through the alleys like projectiles. anyone who hadn't run away in time had almost no chance of surviving. the third death zone was the area around the phi phi princess and charlie hotels. there, too, the whole area was swept bare. that was where the dead were mostly tourists.

a tsunami information center was built at the edge of the phi phi princess compound. it displays photographs of the destroyed island and gives information about the sequence of events during the disaster. i have never been able to find an accurate total number of people who died here. the lowest number i found was 1500, but most people i talked to spoke of 2500 or even 3000 dead. hundreds of people are still unaccounted for.

the information of hi phi phi, the tsunami aid organization, seems the most credible to me. it states that after the tsunami, 850 corpses were found on the island. in addition, approximately 1300 people are still missing. most of them were washed out to sea. for months afterward, body parts – sometimes identifiable – still floated up onto the beach.

after a reading at northwestern university north of chicago, a listener once told me that a resident of evanston by the name of ben abels had lost his life in thailand. the listener thought he remembered that abels had been on phi phi island. i did some research and found out that he had even stayed near us in the phi phi princess, in bungalow 155. his girlfriend, elizabeth, survived with an injured arm and a shattered leg that was saved by an eight-hour operation. ben abels remained missing for a long time. his family employed two private agencies and a forensic laboratory, which searched his room for fingerprints in order to compare them with those of body parts found in thailand. their intensive efforts to find their son's remains bore no fruit for months. in march, 2005, however, bits of torso and head washed ashore that, thanks to dental evidence, could be identified as ben abels's remains.

13

my walk of christmas day, 2004 led me past the irrigation water reservoir and up a small hill to another bungalow compound. beside it was a dusty, burnt-out meadow, where kids played soccer in the afternoon heat. for a moment i wondered if we shouldn't stay here during our second week. but the whole place seemed too grubby and too far from the ocean.

i came to a mosque. mhad tanmakala, the imam of koh phi phi, lived here. his parents belonged to the first six muslim families that settled the island sixty years ago. they established its palm plantation on the narrow strip of land. the father was the first imam of koh phi phi. he had lived through the radical change on the island in the eighties, when its two falafel shops were replaced by hotels, restaurants, and bars, and a new morality was ushered in: alcohol, prostitution, pork. mhad tanmakala considers the tsunami as righteous punishment for the island's depravity. i read this in a report that alexander osang prepared for the spiegel, but which never got printed, because journalistic enthusiasm for the tsunami had died down.

the tourist life of ton sai bay began right behind the mosque. i strolled past the street vendors and massage parlors until i came to a travel bureau. that gave me the idea of asking about lodging for our second week. perhaps they had simple private quarters to offer. i took off my sandals at the entrance, walked up the two steps to the open office area. a man and a woman sat at their desks, dealing with other customers. i had to wait. a workman was busy installing a new telephone connection.

everything here moved at a snail's pace. when the woman made a phone call, the man couldn't use his phone, and vice versa. but i didn't have anything else to do, so i looked at a couple of travel brochures and observed the people on the street.

a thai fellow came around the corner with a baggage cart, followed by two men, by all appearances father and son. they attracted my attention because at first glance i thought the father was my danish friend claus clausen. i quickly realized my mistake but the similarity was nonetheless astonishing. this man was also a scandinavian in his mid-fifties, and he still wore his hair, already quite gray, on the long side, which was typical of an old '68er. in addition he had a three-days' growth of beard, and looked very well-dressed in linen slacks and open-necked shirt.

the young man at his side wore skater shorts and had long blonde dreadlocks. father and son, i assumed, together on vacation, and now on their way to their lodgings. they were chatting and laughing. i watched them go by and had the feeling that they were both doing everything right. i envied them a little bit and didn't quite know why.

two days later i saw them again, at the bar of the maritime park hotel in krabi. late in the evening we had found lodging on mattresses in the dining room. a doctor had given us some valium. i didn't take my pills right away, but went for a walk instead. everywhere i went i met desperate people who had lost family members. i spoke with some of them. then i went to the hotel bar, still in my green iowa shirt; i didn't own any other clothing. a couple of hours earlier i had washed the t-shirt at a faucet in a buddhist monastery. now it didn't stink quite so powerfully of sewage. the huge television screen at the bar carried the cnn reports of the tsunami. i watched it for a while. i would have loved a beer, but i couldn't order anything because i had no money. then i spied the scandinavian with his dreadlocked son off to the side behind me. it was good to see them again.

i told them that i had watched them on phi phi island. the man said that he had come to phi phi on his private boat and only meant to stay one night. as they left the next morning, the wave caught up with them on the way back to krabi. when he saw it coming from behind, he swerved the boat around, yelled to his son to throw himself down on the deck, and then, with great good luck, rode up over the wave.

my '68-er was a swede. unlike my friend claus clausen, he was no leftist intellectual, but rather a prosperous businessman. i liked him anyway. not just because he bought me a beer.

when i came back to the darkened dining room where at least 200 people lay on the floor it was difficult to find our spot at first. there was just dim emergency lighting, so i blundered around among the many bodies, annoyed that i hadn't taken better note of our location. when i finally found our mat i saw that edith and children were fast asleep. i took the valium, lay down, and burst into tears.

14

the scandinavian and his son had long since disappeared with their luggage cart when the travel bureau employee finally found time to pay attention to me. after several phone calls he explained that everything on phi phi was booked for the next week. he didn't think he would be able to find any private rooms. he showed me catalogues with lodgings on neighboring islands. mostly these were pictures of bungalow resorts. i read the descriptions, tried to assess the places based on the pictures, and finally decided on accommodations on lanta island. the man telephoned and found out they were reserved. i chose a different hotel on lanta island; this time it worked.

the man insisted that i make up my mind immediately, but i wanted to talk with my family first and wait for an offer from our hotel. he was visibly annoyed when i put on my sandals and left. i don't know what happened to him. on the following day the travel bureau was out of my range, far beyond the mountains of debris. a year later it was nowhere to be found.

when i returned to our hotel at the end of my christmas walk, the receptionist whom i had admired when we checked in the day before gave me a letter with lodging options for an additional week. no matter what, we would have to change bungalows. our choices included two of the cheapest row bungalows, which weren't next to each other, or a luxury bungalow combined with a row bungalow. i set off for the beach, found edith under a tree, and began to discuss living arrangements for our second week with her. we didn't reach a conclusion, not even when we went to a bar for happy hour and compared our offers over mojitos. maybe, we thought, we should do what dominika's parents had – take a trip along the coast in a long-tail boat to see if we could find private lodgings. maybe we would even find the hippie resort to which i had sent those emails and never heard back.

while we were weighing our options in this bar, our children were exploring the cheap cds and dvds available in the bustling alleys. elias found a complete edition of the tv series friends, which we used to watch together every evening during our year in new york, but he couldn't just go ahead and buy it. his money was locked in the safe.

15

on the morning of december 26th edith woke up around eight o'clock because she thought she felt the room quaking. before she was awake enough to take a look around, there was no longer any trace of shaking. she thought it might have been an earthquake. years ago she had experienced one in vienna. she had awakened in the middle of the night. in the morning the news carried the story of a weak earthquake that nobody else in our circle of friends had even noticed. edith wasn't alarmed. since she was lying awake, without reason, it seemed, she took the opportunity to go to the toilet. then she came back to bed to catch another forty winks.

the phi phi princess served breakfast only until ten o'clock. at first we found that annoying. but apparently it had to do with the fact that there wasn't a separate breakfast room and the restaurant had to set up the noontime buffet promptly. we doubted that our children would make it to breakfast. when we had left our terrace at one a.m. and pulled the curtains they weren't even back yet. they called edith at nine-thirty. sophie came home first. elias wanted to sleep a little while longer, but then came along anyway because he was afraid he might not find the path to the dining pavilion. we had been there for breakfast only once before, on the previous day.

there were only a few hotel guests eating breakfast in the beach restaurant. on this morning edith and i had upset stomachs, without really knowing the cause. we had eaten well on christmas eve and christmas day, especially fish and seafood dishes. maybe it would be appropriate to go easy on the salads. i ate a little and drank my coffee without much enthusiasm. we didn't know anybody. emine and claude weren't here. the day before we had seen them at breakfast and again in the evening. at the next table there sat a heavy, almost bald, white man with a thin thai woman. they were speaking german together. i couldn't help thinking of the sketch by gerhard polt, in which a german discusses his thai girlfriend as though she were a sweet little puppy.

the first swimmers had begun to settle down on the beach under the mangrove trees and palms. some were on lounge chairs that didn't belong to the hotel and they had to pay extra for them. most just lay on beach towels. a man set his little daughter down into one of those huge tricycles that float, and he pushed her back and forth in the water. the tide was in. there were only light waves on the ocean. it was going to be a beautiful day for swimming.

elias and sophie told us how they had spent the evening. first they were in the monkey bar at the end of lohdalum bay and later, because things were fairly quiet there, they went to the reggae bar. reggae bar, that sounded good. that's where i wanted to go.

we talked about where we would spend the second week. i reported on the offers so far. we shouldn't extend our stay here, i said, but rather, as we had originally agreed, look for something cheap instead. at that point sophie turned to elias: you're the one who talked us into all this, otherwise we could just stay here in this beautiful hotel. and then edith said elias should please show some initiative and take part in our search. for example, he could go to the pier when ships arrived to see if anybody were offering lodgings there. this idea did not appeal to elias in the least. i added another one. why not go to the reception desk and have that safe opened for you?

today i'm very glad that he went neither to the pier nor to the reception desk.

shortly after ten o'clock a few young people came into the restaurant, the last breakfast guests. we talked about what we would do today. perhaps take an excursion along the coast in a long-tail boat. but not until later. first i wanted to wait to see how this upset stomach was going to develop. the waiters sat down at a nearby table and began to have their breakfasts. we left the beach restaurant and returned to our bungalows without noting that the water was receding. edith lay on the bed; she had a stomach ache. i picked up the hotel brochure, sat down beside her, and read aloud about the activities that were offered. you could go jogging along the beach in the morning and you could do yoga. the door to the terrace was open a crack. suddenly we could hear noise outside. people were running past. edith said, here come the joggers. i looked outside and what i saw upset me: it was mostly locals running. among them, many hotel employees in their uniforms. i went out onto the terrace. the people running by shouted something that i did not understand. suddenly it was clear that these people were in panic. they were running for their lives. in the meantime edith had joined me on the terrace. we stood there rooted to the spot and didn't understand what was happening. today i imagine that someone waved, or shouted to us that we should run too.

something has happened, i said, but i had no idea what it could be. next door i saw sophie standing on the terrace. i called to her, both of you come quickly. we have to run.

and then, behind the people running past us i saw water flowing. not even knee deep. it didn't seem threatening. it flowed along the path, but the people were running as if there were some completely different threat. fear was etched in their faces. they were all screaming. sophie went and got elias out of the bungalow.

quick, quick, i yelled. we have to run.

now the water wasn't flowing along the path anymore. it was coming up over the grass and the garden beds. we ran after the other people, first along the path to the left, then to the right, toward steps that led to the terrace of a two-story building. this structure was attached to our reception hall. it was a storage and administration area for the phi phi princess hotel. behind it was a passageway about three meters wide, and behind that, the four-story phi phi hotel. when we reached the stairway of out hotel's administration building it was already overcrowded and more people kept pouring in from all sides. they clustered in front of the steps. we shoved and got shoved but didn't make any progress. screams could be heard from the beach, which wasn't far, maybe a hundred meters. you couldn't see it because there were bungalows in the way.

i looked back and suddenly saw the water coming, swirling toward us between the bungalows. people were rushing to the stairs. hurry! i cried, hurry! our children were to my right. sophie was a little bit farther ahead, already close to the stairway landing, with elias behind her. in the melée, as people forced their way toward the steps, sophie got shoved aside. she screamed, i'm being crushed! elias was shoved in the other direction. i kept calling hurry! but there were simply too many people. nothing moved. we were already standing in water. it wasn't deep yet, maybe twenty centimeters. edith was behind me on my left. someone had forced his way between us. the water got loud. i turned around. i still experience what happened next in slow motion: not a mighty, towering wave, but a foaming, rapidly rising tide that slips in among the objects it has surrounded and just keeps coming toward us. i said to edith, this is going to get really, really bad. around us the cries and the throng – everyone wanted to climb these stairs as fast as possible. edith said, stay with me! somebody got between us. i stretched my arm out and we took each other by the hand. at that moment the rolling wave had a powerful pull, like a fast-rising flood. it lifted us up and carried us up the stairs.

edith recalls that she looked over to the children and took comfort that they were close together. the steps, which had just been crammed with people, were suddenly empty. i kept holding edith's hand. with my free hand i tried to grab the railing, but i couldn't get a grip. we were washing along. for a moment i thought i could just step out onto the cement half-landing and keep going up the stairs that led in the other direction. but now the water was rising so fast and with such a powerful current that i couldn't find my footing. i tried to hold tight at the cement landing, which was still sticking up out of the water as we were washed toward it. as i reached for it, it too, disappeared underwater. i anchored myself to the baluster by hooking my knee around it.

up to this point i had the feeling that i could do something. i was not just a victim of the situation. now i realized how powerless i was. i lost my grip on edith's hand. the water pushed me back over the concrete balustrade and washed over me. i was suddenly submerged and realized that it wasn't just water, but waves of objects that were smacking me. i had to unhook my knee and let go of the cement balustrade.

when i came up for air, i didn't see edith anymore. but i saw other people in the water. it was filled with wooden wreckage and corrugated metal. the wall of the phi phi hotel

was a bottleneck, and the accumulated debris in the wave came
at us relentlessly as it washed into the alley between the hotel
and the administration building. i remember half a bungalow
roof, which people had climbed onto, coming toward me. i
reached for it and tried to climb up too, but there were already
too many people on top. the roof tipped toward me and
pushed me underwater. i was torn away by a whirlpool of mud
and debris. when i was underwater, everything around me
swirled as if i had fallen into a mixer. i kept getting hit by
pieces of wreckage, and then, briefly, tossed up to the surface
again, only to be dragged down by an undertow. i couldn't see
anything, got water in my mouth, and suddenly couldn't tell up
from down anymore. at this moment i was gripped by the fear
that i couldn't make it. and then came the clear thought, this is
the end. this realization came as a shock, but it wasn't followed
by despair. it was more like a kind of regret that i couldn't die
some other way instead of perishing here in the muck. it was
the feeling of an absolutely undignified end. by regret i mean a
kind of melancholy parting gaze, because i had created a false
image of life for myself. i had thought that it was about
something. now i saw myself becoming part of the filth that
surrounded me. and i knew that in reality i had never been
anything else. then came the resolve to fight to the end. as long
as you can move, i said to myself, you have to try to get out of
here.

this struggle took place at ceiling height in the phi phi
hotel. somehow i grabbed an electric cable that ran along the
wall and held on desperately. now i had a handhold. i could tell
up from down again, and i could resist the swirling water with
my own strength. i wanted to get to the surface but i couldn't
get any higher. something was on top of me. i tried to push it
aside, but that didn't work. it was a panel that had somehow
gotten wedged into the wall with the other debris. with my
right hand i held onto the electric cable. with my left i tried to
force the obstacle aside. i pushed again and again. i didn't feel
any pain, but i realized that my fingers weren't working. i had

cut several tendons on the corrugated metal. but i did manage to shove the panel aside and surface.

i found myself in the middle of a heap of broken furniture, a mountain of boards, poles, pieces of plastic and metal that had gotten wedged against the wall and clogged together. at least my head was above water; i could breathe. suddenly edith surfaced in this same hole. like me, she had been swept into the whirlpool by the mass of water that had formed behind the stairway, and then carried by the current to the same spot. she, too, had thought the end had come. she had also thought: i am going to have to perish in this filthy water because i didn't make it up the stairs. she thought she was going to lose the children and took small comfort in the fact that they were no longer little. she can remember that everything above her was closed over and she had already given up. and that then suddenly she could stick her head out through a crack and take a gulp of air, and that she was with me. she doesn't know how long she stayed underwater, and i don't know that about myself either. i thought i had used up all my options. staying underwater for one minute is no problem for me, so it must have been a minute or less. i certainly didn't have the chance to prepare with a really deep breath. in my memory time seems to have stood still in those few seconds when i thought i was staring death in the face.

16

sophie:
i got ready for the beach. i wanted to go to the tree i had been under the day before. elias went back to bed and i stuffed things into my backpack: camera, a book about che guevara that my girlfriend fabi lent me, forms to register my essay in my major field, a pad of paper and a pen, sunglasses, my mp3 player. i was just getting ready to leave for the day. then i saw these people running past. i stepped back a few paces out of

fear and closed the door again. it looked dangerous because so many people were running by. the first thing i thought was that they were being chased by some animal. then i went back out onto the terrace and looked back at you. you had just yelled: run. we have to run. i went back to elias, who was still in bed. he wanted to put on a t-shirt, i said no, forget it, come on. then we ran after the people, toward the stairway. i didn't know why i was running. at some point i turned around and then i saw a little bit of water. it was flowing along the path. but that didn't look dangerous. then we were in front of the steps and nobody could get any farther. the people pushed and yelled for those in front to move. you yelled too. i turned around and saw you. elias was right behind me and after that i don't know much anymore.

i just realized that all of a sudden i was standing in water and had lost my flip-flops, and that the water kept on rising. for a long time i had just one flip-flop, the other was gone. at first that was important to me, not to lose the flip-flops. and then the water rose higher and higher. i pulled myself up over the railing. i climbed hand over hand up to the next landing. while i was climbing i lost my backpack. the water rose fast, and i saw my backpack floating. it had gotten stuck under me at the landing and i had taken it off quickly before it washed away. finally the whole stairway was underwater, and i didn't see any of you anymore. there were people there, an american guy others too. they stared out at the water. so did i. but i don't remember what i saw. i don't have an image of it anymore, it's just gone.

there were a lot of people on the terrace. but suddenly there were fewer. they had started to climb up higher, onto the roof. and then i saw you on the wall of the phi phi hotel. we called to each other. but elias wasn't there.

then you could see the second wave in the distance. the american tried to calm me down. i asked how high it was. and the american said, it'll go down soon. and then i caught a glimpse of elias. he had pulled himself up to us from somewhere. suddenly there he was. then i climbed onto the landing, because i wanted to see up the stairway. i hoped it would go a lot higher, but there wasn't much to it, just this landing. and then the wave came, and i saw that it was bringing everything with it. all the garbage, filth, and stuff. and then i was really scared, that it would sweep us away and sweep you away. but it didn't. it came very close to washing over the terrace. there was a child lying there, and they were giving it mouth to mouth. it was a very small child. and there were people lying in the rooms, with others trying to take care of them.

then elias and i climbed onto the roof together. but the roof was very hot. neither of us had any shoes. a woman threw shoes over to me from the phi phi hotel, flip-flops, but they were way too small for me. elias was still barefoot, he couldn't stand it on the hot roof. i took off my t-shirt so he could stand on it.

there was a father with his daughter, they wanted to string bed linen between our top floor and the phi phi hotel. we didn't know how we could get over there. there were people at the windows and on the balconies. they wanted to help us and had tied the sheets together. i had a little water bottle in my backpack. so i drank some water and gave some to the man and his daughter. then i watched them pull you up to the third floor.

we drove ourselves crazy trying to figure out how to get over to you. somebody or other had brought mattresses from the rooms and thrown them down onto the garbage heap so that the people from the hotel could climb over that way. you kept calling, that we should climb over. but i didn't want to. i was so afraid of falling off. i just wanted to get up higher. i would have liked it best if the bed linen had reached all the way across, but that hadn't worked.

finally we got off the balcony. elias had no shoes. he climbed down barefoot. and someone shoved a baby into my hands. i didn't want to take the baby because i was worried about getting across. but someone just gave me the baby. he said i should take it and showed me how to get over. he had something else to do, i don't know what. whatever, i suddenly had a little naked baby in my arms. the man showed me how to cross over the mattresses. on the other side a woman took the kid from me. we climbed through a window into a horrible room, in which everything was destroyed. i wanted to climb up as fast as possible, as high as possible. down below there was mud and filth. the stairs were full of blood.

17

elias:
   i don't like to talk about it. because i still have bad dreams about it. especially when i go into detail. when i've told friends about it, it has always happened that at night i've dreamed of the wave or disaster in the family.
   i lay down in bed after breakfast. i wanted to catch a little more sleep and then go to the beach later. suddenly sophie got all hyper and stressed, that something was up and we had to beat it. when i was outside you yelled, run, run, and then i saw that other people were running. as i was running i saw the water flowing behind us. and i thought, shit, everything's going to be flooded and we won't be able to get back into our room for a while. but i never thought that the wave could sweep us along with it. i was even surprised that the people were in such a hurry. it looked like such a tiny flood. i was mad that i had left the door open and that now everything would be under water. i even wanted to run back and close the door. all the fast running and the people screaming on the beach made me panic. a lot of people were yelling, but i still couldn't tell why; it was something or other coming toward us, but it was hard to understand why the people were screaming about a little bit of water flowing around the bungalows.
   but suddenly i was up to my knees in water and it was

rising quickly, i felt the pressure and realized that a real wall of water was coming toward us. i stood there and basically couldn't do anything. the stairs in front of us were jam-packed. the people forced me back. that made me panic. i knew i had to get up there, but there was no way. i tried to do what sophie had done and climb up. i was really upset that she was already upstairs and i couldn't follow. that was something that happened a lot when i was a kid: sophie could do a lot of things better. that suddenly occurred to me. and those were my last thoughts before the water swept me away. then everybody was screaming.

i can remember two men saying: let's go into the tunnel. i saw some kind of space under the stairs. i don't know for sure what it was. probably just the ground floor in back. i saw a couple of men go in there, maybe to relieve the water pressure. let's go into the tunnel. that's what i understood. they were in there, and i thought, not me, thanks. i'm going to wait and see what happens. these were split-second thoughts. i just saw sophie jump over the railing, heard the voices saying let's go into the tunnel, and then the big wave was there and it washed me along with it.

unlike you, i definitely wasn't swept up the steps. for a long time i wasn't sure about that, but when i saw the pictures you showed me, i was certain that i had been swept to the left of the stairway and behind the building into the same passage as you. only you had to go over the stairs and i was carried right around the corner. and you didn't get into this current until after me with all the corrugated tin and stuff. i was pulled underwater and didn't come up – not because there was a roof on top of me, but because the whirlpool held me down. it was like what i knew from the atlantic when a wave pulls you underwater and you can't surface for a while. but then i actually did come up again and took a deep breath. that seemed to be the smartest thing to do. whenever i surface i take a deep breath. and then somebody underwater grabbed me and pulled me back down. someone caught hold of my feet and pulled. i thought, shit, this is like on the titanic. i remember the scene where kate winslet gets pulled underwater by somebody who panics. anyway, i was suddenly underwater again and realized that someone was pulling himself up on me, using me to save himself, and i went down. and then i was afraid of dying. i thought, i'm never going to do this, i'll never get to the surface. but then the water calmed down, maybe because it backed up, and i came up again. it was a girl who had pulled me. she had long blonde hair. i brushed the hair and all the muck off her face. she was covered with filth. there was still force there, an undertow, but it was calmer. i said, i think it's over now. it's gonna be okay. and she said, no, nothing is okay and started to cry. somebody stuck a pole down into the water and pulled the girl to the back wall of the building that we originally wanted to climb up on. the water was still moving, like a river. i had to hold on somewhere so as not to get dragged away. i think it was a pipe that i grabbed, a pipe on the wall of the phi phi hotel, but i'm not sure what it was. it had to have been way in the back of the passageway between these two buildings. or maybe i was already around the far corner. in all the mess i couldn't make out where i was. all i know is that i held on so as not to be carried away. there was open space in front of me. it could have been the reception area of the phi phi princess. that's where water poured in and i saw it carrying people along with it. i held on to the pipe. the water flooded in like crazy, with people in it. of course i held on with all my strength so as not to get swept away – that was my biggest worry. and then i saw a child getting dragged along by the current. it was screaming. i thought, he's going to be sucked into that room and drowned. i held on to the pipe with one hand, reached for the child with my other hand, and took him under my arm. he calmed down in my arms and stopped crying. that made me feel good because the child felt safe now. but nobody was taking care of me. they had pulled the girl up and now i was alone with the child. i got this tremendous feeling of panic that now i was going to be swept in there with

the child. i began to yell: i have a child here! on the balcony
above me they noticed me, somebody leaned way over,
grabbed the child's hand and pulled him up. but that wasn't
going to work with me. somebody said i should go over to the
wall of the administrative building where they had pulled the
girl up before. to do that i would have had to cross the river
and i didn't dare. i was afraid my knee would give out. there
was a lot of pressure in the water and my knee used to give out
a lot. i panicked again,. the girl got saved and so did the child,
but nobody's saving me, i thought. they wanted me to get to
the wall so they could pull me up. but i didn't dare let go of the
pipe and was afraid because of my knee. then they held a pole
out to me and pulled me to the wall. from there i climbed onto
a balcony. they were resuscitating a child that wasn't moving.
but it wasn't the same child i had saved, because they had
pulled him up at the hotel. then i went through the room and
looked for you. there were tons of people in this room, a lot of
blood and screaming. then i got to the terrace and wandered
around, when suddenly i ran into sophie coming from the
other direction. and sophie said you were okay. i didn't see you
until i was on the roof. i was holding on to sophie, we stood
there and shivered, and then the next wave came. i could see it
coming in from the ocean. except for a couple of palm trees
there was nothing left standing. all the houses were gone. it
wasn't a classic wave, like the ones in the movies, it was like a
wide river coming toward us. the water rose fast. all the trash
was swept in again. people were climbing up palm trees. in my
memory i imagine that one tree had little crossbars. and
somebody climbed up when the new wave was visible in the
distance. high up there he was safe. someone else climbed up a
normal palm tree, and he made it. a third man, a tourist, didn't
make it. he just stood there, and i thought, run, do something,
try to climb up, but he just stood there and got swept along by
the wave and sucked down into the water. then the water rose
and came right up to the terrace. sophie and i and other people
climbed onto the low wall. later we climbed onto the roof.

then we saw you standing over on the opposite side. a couple of men made big holes in the roof. i didn't know what that was for. in another building we looked at, the roof tiles had also been broken through.

even though it was hot up there on the roof, i didn't want to come down because i was afraid of a new wave and because i had seen how it had swept that man away. you called out that we should come over to you, you'd see whether a new wave was coming. but i didn't dare go down. when we were down on the terrace again a man talked to sophie. she said, no, no. i though he wanted something sexual, but all he said was he'd help us get across if we would do him a favor. he didn't give up. then we went with him. he just wanted sophie to carry an injured child that was lying in a room over to the phi phi hotel, which she did. then the man showed us the way across. he and others had thrown mattresses onto the piles of debris so that you could climb over more easily. sophie had the child by the hand but still didn't want to climb over the mattresses. but you called and told her to come over, and she did. we climbed into the phi phi hotel through some window or other. a woman took the child from sophie. it was a horrible room, full of garbage and filth. from there we climbed a few steps to the second floor where many injured people were lying. that was the first time i walked through pools of blood. i was still barefoot. there was so much blood on the floor. walking through this blood, i had a song by coldplay going through my head: we live in a beautiful world. it kept repeating in my head like a tape loop.

we ran through the entire hotel looking for you. upstairs, downstairs, everywhere. we looked in every hallway, every corner. we just couldn't find you. we looked and looked. and then we saw people going up on the flat roof. and i said, sophie, come on, it's useless, let's go up on the roof and wait there. they'll look for us. if everybody searches, we're bound to miss each other. i calmed sophie down, because she had started to cry. she thought, you wouldn't show up and, well . . .

i said that you'd definitely show up because you had survived. we had seen you. sophie just kept crying, and i held her and tried to calm her. i don't know what was going on around us. i was just paying attention to sophie. we sat down on this roof in the shadow of a water tank and waited. sophie wanted to keep looking, but i said: no, we're waiting. and we waited a pretty long time. for sophie it seemed longer than for me; i was focusing on calming her down. and then suddenly we saw you. that was fantastic. it was insane. that you made it too, and we were all together again. and then we all hugged and cried.

18

a year later, it isn't very easy to find the place where bungalows 240 and 242 used to stand, because there's nothing left of them. we wander in a pile of gravel and sand overgrown with vines and flowers and try to make out the area where we stayed by estimating the distance to the pool, the ocean, and the administration building. in a few places you can still make out rubble from concrete footings under the vegetation. about a third of the palms still stand. most have lost their leaves; they're just dead stumps now. since we were here, new palms have been planted around the two tennis courts of the neighboring cabana hotel, which is about to reopen. on the day of the tsunami this place was cleared. it offered the best site for helicopters to land. it was the center of hope. here the severely injured waited for transport off the island. here the nurses landed. the chaos was organized from this place. here the swede, erik, and cici, the woman from trinidad, led the operation. they coordinated the rescue effort. without them the strongest, not the weakest, would have gotten the coveted places in the helicopter. erik was no doctor; he was a diving instructor. but he knew first aid. cici was a doctor. she made up the transport lists. erik took care of logistics.

we lived in the shadow of a water tank on the flat roof of

the phi phi hotel. we had nothing else to drink. but i had gotten flip-flops that made it possible for me to walk outside the building.

i met erik on the fifth floor. he was just doing his rounds through the hotel to look for the most seriously injured people. he told us all what to do, and the cooperative ones did what he said. there was a man who needed to be carried out, whose leg had been severed. erik spoke of a helipad, a helicopter landing place. that sounded encouraging. even though we hadn't seen any helicopter yet.

six of us were carrying the man. i could only grab hold with one hand. we carried him in a sheet. if we had put him on a door we wouldn't have gotten down the stairs. the sheet, however, was a very unstable solution. the man, an italian, clenched his teeth, but every now and then he cried out. erik knew where we had to take him. if the helicopter or anybody else were going to arrive, the badly injured would have to be ready right there. a year later several paths cross the compound of the phi phi princess. i try to orient myself among them, but they're not identical with the original paths of the hotel layout. the network of makeshift roads follows the service roads for the backhoes that made their way among the protruding, piled-up concrete foundations.

only three buildings of the phi phi princess still stand: on the beach, there are the pool and the dining pavilion, and also, in the middle of the isthmus, the administration building that we ran toward. this building stands with its long side close to the phi phi hotel. its short side is contiguous to the large reception hall, of which nothing is left but the base of the four-sided fountain that stood in the center. now a pile of rubble stretches between this fountain and the administration building. two workmen are busy sorting through the ruins. it's the last area in the phi phi princess compound where there is still a miscellaneous mass of objects and materials left behind by the tsunami. it's as though a wrecking ball had been hard at work before the inhabitants had moved out. both of the workers – one with a white sunhat, the other, a bandanna on his head – squat in this field of ruins, roof tiles, paving stones, pieces of concrete, broken sinks, iron bars, stones, and occasional household objects washed in among them. they are making piles and exposing objects. a swim fin, a portable radio, a notebook case, a credit card, a sneaker, a t-shirt, a rivet-studded belt, identification papers, a woman's sandal, a lipstick, a watch. they work slowly and show each other the objects before they throw them aside. then they go and lean against the wall of the administration building to have a cigarette. here they find shade, since nothing protrudes from the wall overhead but a remnant of the roof of the reception hall.

i talk to them both, but they understand hardly a word of english. i gesture with my camera. they have no objection to my photographing them. then i depart, but turn around again after a couple of paces because it occurs to me that at least one of these objects in the rubbish dump should be in the photo. so i squat down and take a second photo. in the foreground, a tangled-up belt studded with four rows of rusted rivets. the thai worker in the white hat is in the background.

i can't say why i chose the riveted belt of all things. plenty of other objects were lying around. six months later when we view the film i've pried out of the camera and cleaned, and it turns into a strange situation. in the picture you can just see elias, lying on the prow of a ferry with his t-shirt pulled up. elias is next to me looking at the pictures, and he suddenly cries out, hah, there's my belt! i had completely forgotten i had it in thailand. i've been looking for it ever since.

then i remember this photograph i took a year after the tsunami. i show it to him. that's it, he says, that's my belt. at least it's exactly the same as the one i had.

such coincidences seem meaningful without my being able to say where, precisely, their meaning lies. when i study an old map of the hotel compound, the mystery diminishes slightly. a line drawn from the middle of the bay to the reception hall of the phi phi princess cuts through bungalow 242. that makes it fairly probable that our belongings washed into the reception area of the hotel.

19

when i return i realize the administration building stands much closer to the ocean than i recalled. the confusion stems from the fact that there wasn't this unobstructed view of the beach before. even after the tsunami it wasn't an open space, but rather a landscape of trash piles. continuing farther along in the territory of the former four-star resort, which now teems with wildflowers, we come upon a small pile of sand with a simple cross, just wooden boards nailed together, stuck into it. we don't know whom this memorializes. we look at this cross the way we looked at the corpses a year ago. now, as then, incapable of comprehending what criteria have decided our fates.

we walk back to the administration building hand in hand. this building's outside staircase was where it was decided who would, and who would not, escape the water. mostly, i'm surprised at how narrow the stairs are. two people can just barely pass each other on them. in my memory they seem like a broad, grand ascent to a palace. salvation awaited up there. all hope pointed upward. i recall a large terrace, with room for everybody. in reality it's just a verandah, roughly two meters wide, on the front of the building.

behind the outdoor stairway there are now painters' buckets and construction materials. the roof has been repaired, the ground floor renovated. laundry hangs out to dry on the terrace landing.

people who had no roof over their heads have moved into the administration building of the phi phi princess. a wooden shed has been added on the left, behind which a thai family lives in the most primitive conditions. next to this sits a tall stack of wooden beams, to build further additions.

and then we stand in this passage between the administration building and the phi phi hotel, where the surging water hit us. i see the electric cable that became my lifeline. it runs along the wall at a height of approximately two and a half meters. back then it was under water. on the other side is the ledge that sticks out from the facade of the phi phi hotel, where we spent our most terrifying time. even though we had already saved ourselves, we didn't know if our children were still alive.

here in this alley we worked our way out of the mountain of debris. here we finally reached the surface and could breathe. but we couldn't climb through the opening that i had cleared right away. the water was still moving. it pulled our feet toward the reception hall. beams that bobbed on the surface had gotten stuck between the walls. the remains of bungalows were piled up over our heads and all around us.

on the exterior wall of the phi phi hotel there was a protuberance, a narrow cornice. when we were still caught, a woman helped us up there to save us. edith and i helped each other get out through the opening i had made, and we crawled across the floating debris toward this cornice. edith couldn't make it up there right away. i tried to help her. the low-cut blue top she still had on from breakfast was torn. blood ran down her back. finally we were both standing on this ledge; at least for a moment, we were safe.

we heard screams from all sides: people were still in the water, people who tried to scramble onto floating objects or save themselves by climbing up. then the water calmed, flowed more slowly. where were our children? we couldn't see them anywhere.

the woman next to us on the ledge called to someone who didn't answer. she kept calling out a girl's name. edith asked if she were looking for her daughter. she nodded and kept calling the name, which i have forgotten. on the terrace of the administration building across from us an asian woman began to scream. a lifeless child was passed up the stairs to her. a man began trying to resuscitate the child.

we said nothing. we just watched. edith tugged at her torn shirt. she was wearing her bikini top underneath it. she said, i have to go back and get some new things to put on. i nodded. it didn't occur to me what nonsense she was talking. then i noticed some kind of spot on her cheek. you've got something there, i said, and reached for it. it was a contact lens. she put it in her mouth to clean it with saliva. i pulled her eyelids apart to see if the other contact lens was stuck somewhere, but i couldn't find it. edith inserted the lens into her left eye. as it turned out later, it was the lens for the other eye. it scratched, but edith could see a little better with it. we kept searching for our children.

then i noticed blood running down my left hand. i held my other hand under it because i didn't want to get the building dirty. utter devastation lay below us and i was worried about smearing blood on the light-colored wall. edith pulled off her torn t-shirt and wrung it out. i wiped the blood from the ledge with it and held it under my wound. i inspected my hand more closely. it was bleeding in several places. one after the other i tried to move my fingers and noticed that i couldn't move the ring finger and the little finger. i said, my ligaments have been severed. i have to get to a doctor.

just as edith imagined she could just go get fresh clothes to change into, i imagined i could simply go to a doctor. we couldn't absorb what we were seeing. we couldn't talk about the fact that we might have lost our children – an incomprehensible thought. instead we deceived ourselves into thinking we could do anything we wanted. what are the next logical steps? one would be to go to a doctor and have my torn ligaments stitched. in reality we were totally helpless, in no position to move anywhere.

the blood began to seep through edith's shirt. i held it over the water. the woman who had been calling for her daughter had disappeared. she had crawled along the ledge and been hoisted onto a balcony with a sheet. the sheet still hung there. it looked like a good opportunity for us. i thought, that's not for edith; she doesn't have enough strength in her arms to pull herself up.

the water below us was still now. it sloshed back and forth. then the carpet of debris began to move in the other direction, slowly at first, then faster and faster. there were still people in the water. they were being pulled back into the ocean along with these floating objects. now one could see all the way to the beach, where figures were struggling against the receding current among the boats and house roofs,.

we stood on the ledge of the phi phi hotel and heard the intensifying screams, watched people getting dragged out to sea, and tried to tell whether our children were among them. and then came the moment when edith asked me in desperation: do you see our children? i didn't want her to say it out loud. i shook my head. they've got to be somewhere, i said.

20

edith found sophie first. she was standing on the terrace of the administration building across the way. most of this terrace wasn't visible to us. we couldn't see sophie until she approached the stairway. we called to her: sophie, sophie! she saw us and reached her arms out to us.

do you know anything about elias? we called.

i don't know anything, she called back with tears in her voice. i can't find him.

suddenly a loud scream. the water comes back! we saw the second wave coming at us. people who had just been rescued on the beach were swept up again and hurled into the mountains of debris. the water was a surging flood again. it kept rising.

i was afraid that the administration building across from us, where sophie stood on the terrace, might be swept away. i wondered whether she could somehow cross over to us. our building could definitely take a tougher beating, but there was no chance. sophie called to us that we should get up higher. but we couldn't climb any higher. where we stood, there was no way into the building and no way up. people pulled themselves up onto palm trees. the flood kept rising as new wreckage piled up in front of us and clogged the flow of water between the two buildings. we had missed our chance to climb higher to safety. people were screaming on all sides. the water rose and then stopped, just below our feet.

elias was nowhere to be seen. we stood there, our faces dirty, blood and filth all over our bodies. in our heads, just one thought: we've lost a child. we no longer have twins, but just an only child. the happiness of twins that had been granted to us, wasn't meant to last our whole lives. from birth elias had a movement disorder. some things came to him with more difficulty than to sophie. for years we took him to physiotherapy. i had images of his childhood and youth before me. was all that going to drown on a family vacation just before graduation?

people had punched holes through the roof across the way and also through the roofs of other buildings. bustling activity was evident all around. what are they doing over there asked edith. i looked for an explanation: if the water comes back and rises even higher, they're punching holes so the water can pour through and the roof won't be torn away.

all of a sudden sophie called to us: i just saw elias.

she had climbed onto the roof and looked down to the terrace on the ocean side, which we couldn't see from our vantage point. soon afterwards elias also climbed out onto the roof. someone had bandaged his leg for him.

from then on we just focused on the question of how to get back together with our children. we didn't know how many more waves would come. presumably they would keep on coming. one wave after another. the water was receding again, slowly.

everyone who was still alive tried to get to safety as quickly as possible. now, after the second wave, we thought: a series has started, the ocean is all out of balance. how many more waves would come? how high would they be? was what we had just experienced just the beginning? only now, after the second wave, did I realize that there weren't any more bungalows. the whole residential area around our hotel had disappeared. screaming and crying, people wanted to get from the administration building over to the phi phi hotel. sophie and elias walked back and forth on the sloping roof. water and debris lay between us.

knotted sheets had been strung across from one of the balconies. people wanted to make a kind of suspension bridge. but it didn't work. they didn't know how to do it. on the right, people were being pulled up onto the balcony. the phi phi hotel was the highest building anywhere around here. we crawled along the ledge until we were under the balcony where, after the first wave, the woman who had been calling for her daughter had been pulled up. she was still standing there looking down. she had stopped calling. two men held knotted sheets out to us. edith was at least supposed to try to climb up. over her bikini she was still wearing the turquoise stretch cotton summer dress that sophie had sewn for her. it was torn, smeared with blood, and so tight around her thighs that edith couldn't climb in it. so she tore the dress off and threw it away. then she tried to climb up the sheet but couldn't do it. hold on! one of the men called down from the balcony. then they combined forces and pulled edith up.

then i wanted to climb up, but i couldn't grab hold with my left hand. so they pulled me up too. that started my cuts bleeding again. i stood on their balcony with these two men for a while and let the blood drip off its low outer wall. we were barefoot, and we saw that our legs and feet were also bleeding. we couldn't feel it; we just saw it. the men were both italians. one of the them said we could use the bathroom.

we'll be right back, i called to our children. then i held my right hand under my left and went into the room.

two beds stood against the wall. on one lay a man with bandaged hands, surrounded by two women and another man, who was bandaging his lower thigh. bones stuck out of the wound in several places. i'm guessing they were putting sanitary napkins on the places where muscle had been scraped away, and wrapping it with cushion covers. one of the two women wore a head bandage. the other man had both of his upper arms bandaged. we had no more contact with them later. i believe i remember them speaking together either in dutch or a scandinavian language.

a lot of blood from previous users was still in the bathroom. the water worked. i let it run over the wounds on my left hand, and for the first time saw that there were several parallel cuts, all bleeding. there wasn't another fresh hand towel, so i wrapped my hand in a used one. edith washed her face, took the contact lens out, cleaned it, and put it into her other eye. then she washed my face.

we went back to the balcony. i told one of the italians that i had taken a hand towel. he said that was fine. the water had now completely receded. in lohdalum bay a broad carpet of debris had formed. a landscape of wreckage and puddle lay before our eyes. we called to the children to try getting over to us in the hotel. but they didn't dare come down, for fear of the next wave. some fetched mattresses and threw them onto the pile of debris that connected the administration building with the phi phi hotel.

a women in a bikini came out to us on the balcony. she was looking for someone. and she lit a cigarette. i had stopped smoking two months earlier. while we smoked she told me that she couldn't find her husband. it was at that point that i realized people were milling around here looking for family members. how lucky we were. right in front of us, on the roof of the opposite building, we had our children. it was now just a question of time until they would dare to follow the others and cross over to the hotel on the mattresses. finally sophie came first, carrying a baby in her arms. elias followed her. they climbed over the mountain of debris and disappeared through some kind of entrance we couldn't see from our balcony. we called to them to come up to the third floor, where we would wait for them.

21

we left the italians' balcony. in the meantime the lower thighs of the man on the bed had been wrapped with cloths. we wanted to use the bathroom again, but the water had stopped working. we thanked the italians for their help, said goodbye, and went out into the corridor.

there stood a fully loaded room service cart. edith took a bottle of water and some toilet paper, I took a fresh hand towel. at the moment we had no idea how precious these items were. we would soon regret that we had taken just one bottle of water. but as we helped ourselves, we had the feeling we were taking things we had no right to. this wasn't even our hotel.

with toilet paper, water bottle, and a fresh hand towel we walked up and down the corridors of the third floor. it turned out that there were several stairways and several corridors. we didn't know which stairway our children would come up. the floors were covered with tile, along the walls there ran waist-high wooden paneling. injured people were everywhere. many sat on the floor with their backs against the panels. more and more people came into the hotel looking for places for themselves. from the floor below we heard loud weeping and wailing. our children were nowhere to be found – not in the stairways, not in the hallways. we decided to separate to look for them. edith stayed on the third floor and i went downstairs. maybe they had gotten the wrong floor; maybe it wasn't clearly labeled and they were waiting for us on the floor below. as i went down the stairs i could tell that i was entering a first aid station. all along the corridor, the wounded lay on the floor. they moaned, wept, stared straight ahead. the family members mostly cried louder than the injured. most people didn't have anyone to look after them. and everyone slinking around like me was searching for someone. if only they were here among the injured.

i couldn't find our children, nor could i imagine they would wait for us here. so i went down another flight of steps. this ended in a barricade of debris. nobody could have come up this way.

back on the second floor i walked along the corridor to the central staircase. i was barefoot and tried as best i could to avoid the pools of blood that had formed on the brown floor tiles. at the central stairway, which led down to the reception area, the space broadened out to a fifty square meter foyer furnished with a couple of upholstered chairs, tables, standing lamps, and potted plants. here the severely injured lay packed together on the floor. the upholstered chairs were soaked with blood. they were being used to elevate bandaged limbs. more injured people were being carried upstairs from down below.

i saw all this and couldn't really take it all in. i was looking for my children. that was the only thing that interested me at the moment. i walked back to the corridor and up to the third floor again, where i met up with edith. there was no trace of the children. maybe they were looking for us on a different floor? once more we went through the entire third floor, edith still carrying a role of toilet paper and a bottle of water and me with my fresh hand towel. we passed the room service cart again. it had been completely emptied. in the italians' room a few people were still clustered around the bed with the injured man. others stood on the balcony surveying the chaos and looking out to sea in order to catch sight of the new wave. wherever people gathered in groups there was talk of a new wave.

we walked up another flight of stairs, passed through the corridors, looked into all the open doors. everywhere the same thing: people being bandaged, sitting around, or were searching for someone. we didn't find our children and were gradually getting desperate. when we had searched the whole fifth floor it occurred to us that one of the two stairways led even higher up. we followed it. a pink crib stood on a mezzanine. we walked past it and followed the steps, which got narrower, out onto the flat roof.

22

a year later that crib still stands on the mezzanine. that's its spot. if there is any place on phi phi island deeply etched in our memories, it isn't the phi phi princess, where we stayed, but the phi phi hotel with its flat roof, where we survived. the phi phi hotel became one of the central safe havens on phi phi island.

a year after the insanity that reality had suddenly become, we climb the couple of steps up to the reception area. last year three corpses lay here to the left: a woman, a man, and a child. all three were asian. i couldn't keep my eyes off these corpses. for elias and sophie they were the first corpses they had ever seen. i didn't know at the time that the man lying here was the man i had filmed on the ship. i kept looking at him – his face, his body, the wound in his stomach.

we ask the woman at the reception desk if we might see the roof. she wants to know why. we tell her we spent two days and a night there after the tsunami. the woman is friendly. she says that people keep coming back to see the roof. she gets a man who leads us around and shows us everything we want to see. to the right of the reception area there is a stairway that leads down.

a year ago i went down these stairs a little way to look for water, food, blankets, and other necessities. i came to a big, grim cellar room where the water stood knee-high. laundry was floating in it, along with debris that had washed in through the windows. just past the threshold a woman's corpse lay half out of the water. i turned back around.

we walk up the narrow stairs. on the mezzanine there is an empty space right behind the stairway, a foyer from which a door leads to the manager's office. i don't remember the sign, but i do remember this door. it was open a crack, the floor was muddy, but the office had not been demolished by the wave. to the left there stood a desk, beside it shelves with ring binders, the bottom row of which was stuck together with dirt. on the floor to the right lay strange plastic cubes about thirty centimeters long on each side. i took one and tore it open. there were fresh, dry bedclothes inside. it was like winning the lottery. i kept coming back here until i had distributed all the packages. these bedclothes were needed by everyone on the second floor and on the roof.

santa clauses kept coming by. one brought cigarettes, another drinks, another beach sandals. i was the santa claus who gave out bedclothes. toward evening there came the divine epiphany: a helicopter. erik was standing on the beach playing the role of air traffic controller. he made it clear to the pilot that a helipad had been prepared for him. but the helicopter hovered over the landing place. in the cockpit people could see men in helmets, looking around. they couldn't comprehend what they were seeing. from all sides, people limped toward the helipad. i immediately began to make my way in that direction. i was limping too. my right knee, the one i had used to hook onto the concrete balustrade, was aching. i had torn a ligament.

the helicopter was still in the air. erik kept waving to it the whole time to land here on the tennis court. as he came down slowly, it was soon clear to us why the pilot had hesitated. he had seen the injured lying near the landing spot. now the rotor blades were whipping up a real prop-wash of sand, sending grains straight into the wounds of the injured. those of us standing around threw ourselves over them to shield them as best we could with our bodies.

erik asked everyone not in need of immediate treatment to be patient. but no one listened. everyone crowded toward the helicopter. with great difficulty a couple of the most severely injured were loaded into the first machine. when it took off, i heard a german say to his son: when the next helicopter comes you have to scream and scream and don't stop until you're inside. the boy nodded. he had a foot injury.

erik's loud, persuasive voice managed to bring some order to the next transport. he designated cici, the doctor from trinidad, as the authority for determining the boarding sequence.

who are you? asked the german.

i am erik, the swede answered. i am the one who handles the traffic.

on the first evening a helicopter landed four or five times. by nightfall the lounge on the second floor of the phi phi hotel was sparsely populated. one injured man had died before darkness fell. his body lay in front of the staircase all night. at midnight, when i wanted to go to be bandaged, i tripped over it. people had lit a fire at the bandaging station; cici cared for the injured by its light. but there were too many people in line, so i went back. i didn't want to leave my family alone for too long. and once i had returned i didn't want to go downstairs a second time. i had a horror of the darkness in the corridors. you had to feel your way and were constantly stumbling over bodies. emine and i didn't try it again until sunrise.

today, on the right side of the foyer in front of the office where i had found the packets of bedclothes, there hangs a picture of the king of thailand. in front of it there is a little table set with fresh food and drink – cups, vases, red candles. on the floor, more vases with flowers. perhaps this arrangement was there before the tsunami too, and had just been swept away by the water.

on the afternoon of december 26th, last year, on this very spot where today the good spirits are invoked for the emperor, head of the buddhists in thailand, someone had placed a dead woman. soon afterwards the corpse of a man whom i had talked with a bit earlier joined her.

the first time i came down from the roof into the second floor foyer, i knelt down beside a man who had been placed there with nobody to look after him. his face was pale and he had difficulty breathing, but no external injuries were visible. he was asian. i took his hand and asked him in english whether he was in pain. he did not answer. i told him that help would soon come. a helicopter would take him to the hospital. there they will find out what was wrong with him, they would treat him, and everything would be alright again. while i spoke and stroked his hand, he stopped groaning. he was listening to me. i don't know if he understood me. when i came back a bit later – because there were so many glass splinters in front of the hotel that, barefoot as i was, I couldn't leave the building – i knelt down by the man again. he was already dead. when i came by the next time, his corpse had been placed against the wall and covered over. later someone managed to carry it down a half-story to the open place by the stairway. there it lay in front of the door to that manager's office where i had gotten the boxes with fresh bed linens.

the dead attracted the dead. in any case, the living needed to put them together. this little space in the mezzanine became a collection point for those who hadn't made it from the phi phi hotel to the loading area for the helicopter in time.

23

as the employee of the phi phi hotel leads us out onto the roof, it starts raining. it's slippery underfoot. the tanks, the heat exchangers, and the tilt-mounted solar panels stand in rows the way they did a year ago. it could be that a couple of water tanks have been added. the roof of the phi phi hotel was, despite the extreme heat typical of this climate, a desirable refuge for those of us who had no other options. pipes ran across the surface a few centimeters above the roof, so with every step you had to be careful not to trip and get caught in them. people were lying or sitting among all these containers, pipes, and cables. in two places there were structures on the roof, four columns each with a four-cornered pointed roof on top. underneath stood water tanks. one of these pointed roofs stood right opposite the stairway. and there, after seeking them throughout the whole hotel, we finally saw our children sitting. leaning against a water tank. elias held sophie in his arms. they got up and came over toward us. both had bloody arms and legs. but that was all.

we sat down with them in the shady spot at the water tank. we could start a new life with them. we had toilet paper, a bottle of water, a fresh hand towel, and sophie had her backpack. she emptied it out to dry her things. there lay a couple of tampons, a compact mirror, lip gloss, a waterlogged che guevara book, an address book, a pen, a couple of soaked pieces of paper and a digital camera, which no longer worked. because the warranty period hadn't yet elapsed, i returned it later, but got it back with a note that said water had gotten into it, so it wasn't protected by the warranty.

two french couples had settled down beside us. one of the women was pregnant. the four had their backpacks with them. they had come from phuket for a daytrip to the island with the same passenger ship that was later overtaken by the wave in ton sai bay. when they reached land, at first they strolled along the harborside. then they came back and followed the gently sloping alley that led past the phi phi hotel and the phi phi princess to lohdalum bay. at the moment when they passed the entrance to the phi phi hotel they heard loud screaming and saw people running from the harborside in their direction. big wave! someone yelled. they ran into the hotel, past the reception desk, to the stairway, and waited to see what would happen. when the water came all they had to do was run upstairs. they remained unharmed.

the pregnant frenchwoman, who lay beside me on the roof asked me about the thick bandage on my left arm. i unwrapped my hand and showed it to her. she pulled out a little bottle with some antiseptic out of her cosmetics bag. i held the cuts open and she drizzled disinfectant into my wounds. maybe we should have done it more thoroughly, but i didn't want to use up the whole bottle. there were others here who needed it far more. and perhaps it was already too late to prevent an infection. the pregnant frenchwoman's boyfriend had a swiss army knife in his backpack. with the tiny scissors i cut up the clean hand towel and made myself a new bandage. i bound the little finger, the ring finger, and the middle finger together. they had become useless anyway. during the separation and disinfection the cuts had started to bleed heavily again, and so this new bandage was soon soaked with blood.

at the edge of the flat roof there was a low wall, one-and-a-half meters high. a metal handrail ran along its top. most people stood at this railing, looking down onto the chaos below and waiting for the next wave. the rumor that new waves were coming persisted until the next day.

across from us sat an english-speaking woman with a deep cut in her ribcage. her left breast had been severed. she was in pain. later cici found her and had her taken to the helipad. she was airlifted out that evening on one of the first planes.

on the other side, right at the wall, there lay a thai mother with several small children. they were mourning their father. but a small stout man was carried over by two other thais. his leg was bound up. his foot wrapped in a cloth. when he appeared, the whole mood of the family changed. now they were crying with joy that he was still alive. the man's face was pale and he groaned all night. his wife whimpered the whole time. elias lay next to him. he told me later he was afraid the man would die right there. on the next day we made someone on erik and cici's team aware of him and helped carry him to the helipad.

when somebody responsible for the people without shoes

brought a bag of beach sandals up to the roof, i was finally able to look around outside. the countless glass shards and pieces of rusty metal that lay all over the ground were no longer a problem. of course edith and sophie didn't want to just let me go. but i wanted to do something, i couldn't just sit around and wait. my right hand had gotten a few scratches but was otherwise unhurt. at the entrance to the phi phi hotel i passed by the three corpses that were already quite familiar to me, and went down the steps to the alley. i didn't get far, the alley was barricaded. the buildings were still standing on this side but the shops contained everything except what they used to sell. on the other side the booths had collapsed and piled up into a great heap, which blocked the alley to ton sai bay. the reception hall of the phi phi princess had fallen in to the right of the phi phi hotel, and another impassable pile of debris had formed on top of these ruins. to get away from here, it looked as though we were going to have to exit through the windows and balconies we had used to enter the hotel.

i looked around for water bottles. in the pile of detritus a little black lacquered box lay on the ground in front of me. i turned it over. it was a display box with a plexiglas top, the sort jewelers use. its velvet grooves were filled with silver rings. there wasn't a single empty spot. the display box came from a store diagonally opposite the phi phi hotel. the store was destroyed of course, but still recognizable. i placed the box with the rings on top of the store's debris pile so the owner could see it as soon as he returned.

then i turned right to the lobby of the phi phi princess and climbed over beams and steel girders to get closer to this pile of ruins, then i saw two thais looting a travel bag. one found a wallet in the side pocket, took the bills out, and threw the wallet away. the other pulled underwear out of the travel bag and buckled a belt under his t-shirt. i was suddenly very frightened that these two might notice me. there were enough corpses here; one more wouldn't make much difference. the fact that there was a way through these ruins that made it

possible to get to the cabana hotel and ton sai bay became
clear to me the next time i ventured out, when i helped carry
the italian with the severed leg. while doing so we passed the
jewelry shop. the display box with the silver rings had
disappeared.

24

we carried the man over a footpath that led diagonally
through the devastation, through open ditches and over
uprooted palm trees. whenever we had to climb over obstacles,
the man we carried in our sheet began to scream. among the
bearers were two more italians, who spoke soothingly to him.
later, boards were placed over the most uneven places, to make
them more passable. on the first day there were still a lot of
puddles along this path. body parts stuck out of them and the
surrounding piles of debris. some corpses also lay out in the
open. the europeans took care of the injured; the muslims of
phi phi island immediately collected the corpses.

the nets and fences around the tennis courts had presented
no significant resistance to the water, so there were no large
debris heaps there, just a few individual pieces strewn around,
among them parts of boats. a couple of men helped clear the
tennis courts. we set the italian down on one of the mattresses
that had been brought from the cabana hotel. there wasn't any
medical help yet. people had bandaged the limbs of the badly
injured and applied some clumsy emergency dressings. those
who found the first aid cupboards in the hotels were the ones
who had emptied them out. erik approached a man on a
mattress and listened to his breathing. then i heard him say to
an injured person lying beside him: tell me if your neighbor
stops breathing. on the way back to the phi phi hotel i saw a
woman with a blood-smeared face sitting on the ground
staring apathetically straight ahead. i bent down and touched
her on the shoulder. she looked at me and greeted me. it was

emine. she said they couldn't find claude. i invited her up to the roof with us. she got up and i offered her my arm. she spoke french with a swiss accent so i had difficulty understanding her.

they hadn't heard the water coming. claude was in the bathroom at the moment. the first wave tore the bungalow from its foundations and wedged claude's foot. he couldn't get free anymore and he called to emine, telling her to run. she hesitated a moment, then ran outside. everything was already full of water, and she was swept along with it, she couldn't say where. she gestured in the direction of the reggae bar.

emine sat down in the shade of the water tank with us. we had accumulated a small hoard of sheets. later in the afternoon a woman came up to the roof with blue terrycloth bath towels. we grabbed four and still have them in our possession. they bear the phi phi hotel logo. the two frenchmen camped beside us were unhurt. they had brought two sealed cartons of drinks up from the street. one contained cans of red bull, the other, raspberry-flavored soft drinks. they gave elias a can of red bull. he showed it to me and was as happy with it as a little child.

emine had cuts on her head and chest. they had bled heavily but were fortunately not very deep. we bandaged her head with a cut-up sheet and cleaned her face with small amounts of water. she asked if she could stay with us. after a while she said she wanted to search for claude. i offered to go with her. edith begged me not to go too far. i promised. edith then watched us from above as we picked our way through the ruined landscape and examined every body part that stuck out anywhere to see if it were claude's. emine pulled at a red rag. out came a torn dress. it was her ball gown. she had brought it along for new year's eve.

if your dress is here, i said, this is the area we should search. even though we'd been at it for a good two hours and had combed through the whole area around the phi phi princess hotel, we could not find claude. nor did we find any other object that belonged to emine, claude or us. i remember a pile of debris behind the kitchen of the phi phi princess because i just couldn't believe what i saw before me: piles of egg cartons tied together in a bundle. all around, concrete foundations had been torn up, palm trees uprooted, walls toppled, but here lay an industrial-sized package of unbroken raw eggs.

the fact that we couldn't find claude, gave emine hope that he was still alive. during the course of the day we went to the helipad several times to see if he had been brought there. on the beach four men had been carrying corpses on doors they had taken off their hinges and bringing them to a collection point near the cabana hotel. we inspected these corpses too. claude was not among them, nor was he to be found anywhere the following day when evacuation boats came and people gathered by the pier.

in the afternoon, before the bathing towel woman arrived another woman had come to the roof of the phi phi hotel. i don't know who she was, presumably a hotel manager. she said in thai and english that she was going to lead a group of people up the mountain. it was safer there. anyone who wanted to come along should do so. i thought we should go with her. but edith and sophie didn't want to leave the hotel roof. edith said, and if the wave comes while we're on the way? she certainly had a point. before the tsunami it would have taken twenty minutes to reach the viewpoint on foot, but now it would certainly take longer to forge a path to it. about half the people stranded on the roof followed the woman up the mountain. we stayed. from then on we had more room and could lie down and stretch out.

the phi phi hotel had two wings. on one side of the flat roof lived the asians, on the other the europeans. the asian family next to us was an exception, otherwise the people who had fled had grouped themselves neatly by ethnic identity. they stood together in groups, here the europeans, australians and americans, there the asians.

the afternoon sun had significantly reduced the shade on

our spot. we had to huddle close together at the water tank, so as not to be exposed. then our drinks ran out. food was out of the question, but at the very least we needed to drink. the french were not exactly generous with their red bull and raspberry sodas. elias was afraid we would die of starvation and thirst up here.

almost every store in the narrow street had sold drinks. even souvenir and postcard shops had refrigerators with cold drinks. most of the drinks were not in glass, but rather plastic bottles and cans. these still had to be somewhere. we just had to find them.

i suggested to elias that we go downstairs together to scare up something to drink. he came with me. we went past all the misery on the second floor, past the two corpses on the mezzanine and the three corpses in front of the reception desk. the sight of the corpses transfixed elias as much as it did me.

we didn't have to look far before i found a water bottle and another with some mysterious contents. elias found a bottle of blanc de blanc. we took these up to the roof and hid them under the blanket. in the evening a woman brought packets of crackers. we got one roll of crackers for the five of us. aside from breakfast, that was our only meal on this day. our stomach problems had disappeared.

25

on december 7, 2005, we are both feeling a bit queasy aboard a long-tail boat as we approach two new buildings roofed with red tile. for our return to phi phi island we have booked the arayaburi resort on ton sai bay because its bungalows are not on the beach, but twenty to fifty meters above sea-level on the mountainside. one of the buildings with a red tile roof is the renovated hotel restaurant; the other is the newly designed reception hall. several long-tail boats are moored on the beach. a man is bailing water out of his boat with a cut-off plastic bottle. the boatmen are sitting in the shade of a palm tree. as we land on the white sandbank they get up and come toward us. they are joking and peacefully smoking their cigarettes. then they have people hand our luggage across to them and take us to the reception hall. we roll up our trouser legs, hold our shoes in our hands, and climb out of the boat.

long-tail boats lie at anchor on ton sai bay, moored below the beach path with long ropes. with each wave they move a little bit toward the land together, and as the waves recede, they slide back to their old positions. then the ropes pull up out of the sand like tripwires.

there are white plastic tables and chairs in front of the hotel restaurant. on the left stands a demolished backhoe half buried in the sand. behind it is a pile of rusting metal-framed furniture, refrigerators and cabinets. in front of the reception hall, where they had brought our bags, there is a red stone sign: bay view resort. have they taken us to the wrong hotel? everything's fine, says the man, who serves us a welcome drink of papaya juice, the hotel has gotten a new name.

we are driven up the mountain on a steep and narrow concrete path in a little golf cart. with all our luggage, the electric motor gives out. i get out and push. as soon as the path is flat again, i jump on.

the bungalow assigned to us is in one of the back rows. from our terrace all we can see is jungle vegetation and the back sides of other bungalows. we leave our bags and go back to the reception desk. i say that we would prefer an ocean view and that we are prepared to pay for it. the receptionist phones her boss, then says the hotel will upgrade us at no charge. we should choose any bungalow we'd like. most of them are empty anyway. we choose one with a view of the neighboring island, phi phi leh.

no sooner have we moved into our new quarters than it begins to rain. we sit out on the roofed terrace. it's warm, but phi phi leh is no longer visible. the island has disappeared behind a veil of humidity. a bit later the sun comes out for a little while and illuminates the jagged cliff tops in red. soon the leaves on the trees begin to rustle as though a wind were coming up, but it isn't wind, it's a fine, invisible rain, which makes phi phi leh slowly disappear again behind a gray curtain.

the rain stops in the evening. we eat in the hotel restaurant on the beach. the sky is as gray as before. there aren't many guests here. the chef sits down at our table. we ask him about the tsunami's effects on his resort. three tourists were killed. a small shrine wrapped in multicolored ribbons was erected beside a mangrove in their memory. all the employees managed to escape up the mountain in time. the water inundated the reception area and the restaurant, but didn't reach the height of the bungalows. by christmas, he hopes, the resort will be booked full again. it begins to rain again, and we take cover under the roof.

december and january are normally months with little precipitation on phi phi island, but apparently that varies from year to year. during our two week stay a year after the tsunami, there is only one day without rain. we sit on the terrace and read our books. when there's a break in the rain, we go for a walk. soon the open umbrella is hanging in the shower to dry, and we're sitting on our terrace again looking over toward phi phi leh. there is a strange backstory here. i had an indirect connection with this island even before sophie's friend dominika gave us the idea of traveling to phi phi island.

at the press party for the tv film opera ball the director urs egger gave me a book: the beach, by alex garland. he wrote in it: for josef haslinger – another traveler! that was on february 18, 1998. he said he had liked the book so much that he wanted to make it his next film project. he asked me to read it, and if it grabbed me, write a film script, or at least collaborate on one. he asked me that without knowing that the film rights had already been granted to an anglo-american production company, which had given the job to danny boyle, the director of trainspotting. alex garland assigned the scriptwriting to john hodge, who had also written the script for trainspotting. urs egger never even got close to the project. but he didn't know that when he gave me the book. later, on a flight to the u.s., i saw the film, and decided that i liked the novel more than the screen version, which only tells part of the story. ultimately, however, both versions tell about the transformation of what seems like paradise into hell, although not by natural forces.

sitting on the terrace with the film set tangibly in front of me, i get the urge to see the film again. i take the hotel umbrella from the bathroom and for one hundred baht (two euros) buy the dvd in the nearest store. because it's right next to it and because i've always wanted to see this movie musical, i also buy the sound of music. wherever we went in the u.s.a. we used to run into the sound of music. it seems to have been a formative experience for my generation, but in austria hardly anybody knows it.

i come back with the two dvds and we decide not to watch the beach, but rather the sound of music. in the middle of the film edith feels sick to her stomach and has to throw up. from then on she runs back and forth every ten minutes. she breaks out into a cold sweat. her digestion is going crazy.

we have brought immodium capsules with us. she takes two, but throws them up again soon. the sound of music is still onscreen. i keep pushing the pause button so edith doesn't miss anything. the rain drums on the roof, the palm trees and the broad leaves of the jungle trees. edith returns. she wants to keep watching the film.

later a thunderstorm comes up. at the exit to our terrace the wind slaps the curtain back and forth. then it begins to pour and thunder. i am suddenly overcome by the fear of a landslide. haven't we seen it often enough on tv, especially in thailand and indonesia? entire villages covered by an avalanche of mud. our bungalow is built into a steep hill. the pilings of our terrace reach down a good four meters. i strain to listen out into the rain, to notice any unusual noises. whenever the thunder crashes, i think: now the mountainside is going to slide down.

animals are running around on the roof. their pitter patter goes from one side to the other. you can hear the waves crashing against the cliffs. i keep waking up during the night. sometimes because i hear edith when she gets out of bed. now and again i am suddenly wide awake without any reason. i dream that we have cholera and that edith's eyes become glazed over. i keep seeing these slightly upturned, glassy eyes before me. we have jungle fever, i think to myself in my dream, or maybe i'm in a half-waking state. we should never have come back here. last year the tsunami. this year some tropical disease against which we have no vaccinations.

these nightmares accompany me until morning. and always the fear of a landslide. the ground could become so soft that all the bungalows slide into the ocean. i give some thought to the best response to such a situation, but have no idea. there will be a muffled rustling; then the house will start to move; then everything will crash down around us.

it's still raining the next morning. edith says she's feeling better. i turn on the television. on the channel dw-tv there is a report being broadcast called the tsunami – one year later. the camera follows the swedes, camilla, niklas and ulrike andersson, who were orphaned by the tsunami. their father had already died of cancer. their mother had traveled with them to khao lak. it was their first family vacation without their father. when the wave came their mother was in the pool. she drowned in the flooding. the children survived. of all the european states, sweden and germany have the most victims. in all probability five hundred and forty-three swedes died. the corpses of twelve children and five adults were never found,.

camilla, niklas, and ulrike andersson had to sell their mother's house because they couldn't keep it up. they moved into an apartment together. all three were in therapy. in the summer they came back to khao lak and that helped them. they now know, says the oldest daughter, who's maybe sixteen years old, that they didn't do anything wrong. they have nothing to blame themselves for. their mother never had a chance. amateur photos of the tsunami in khao lak are shown in this report. the wave attained a greater height at the beginning, and a much greater speed than the one on phi phi island. you can see the surf several meters high as it crashes into houses and trees. obviously the photo in the spiegel's lead story was taken from khao lak.

at breakfast it's still raining. in the restaurant we run into a french camera crew filming the rain and then fanning out into the town to document phi phi island one year later. despite the constant rain, we leave for a walk. in the morning we notice that tsunami evacuation route signs have been put up everywhere, and there are also white arrows indicating where one should flee. banners give the information that there is going to be a tsunami alarm test at one p. m. tsunami drill, they call it.

when we reach our daily pilgrimage site, the desolate landscape of the phi phi princess, a government delegation approaches us, accompanied by highly decorated policemen, their chests covered with medals that would be fitting ornaments for a military dictatorship. the delegation exits from the dining pavilion that has been temporarily restored for the day-tourists. the hotel manager, these days little more than a ruins administrator, accompanies the delegation toward the harbor. when he returns to the pavilion i speak to him. he says there's a good chance the phi phi princess will be rebuilt.

i say that we stayed here on december 26th. welcome back, he says. you're not the first to have returned. there's going to be a memorial service here on the first year anniversary.

not even he can tell us the precise location of bungalows 240 and 242 anymore, but that's no longer so important to me. in the beginning, the search for locations was a good way to conjure up hidden memories and at the same time see very soberly what was in front of me and what my imagination had added. in the meantime we have crossed over this territory almost daily, and more and more details that i had written in my notes at home have come into focus. we don't have to come back here. we do it almost out of habit. or because we have decided to lay the ghosts in our souls to rest.

i tell the hotel manager about a masseuse, whom i met two days ago. her husband died in the kitchen of the phi phi princess. the manager shows us the kitchen. i glance inside quickly, because the image of all the people trapped in here is unbearable.

26

a year ago the night was bright with stars and the moon was nearly full. the bay lay before us like a ghostly landscape. in front of the cabana hotel, at the collection point for the injured, somebody was tending a campfire. otherwise there was just the light from the sky reflected on the sea. the noise had long since died down. the sea had become quite calm. one could see a series of light gray and dark contours stretching out to the horizon. we thought we could recognize the silhouette of a warship.

three strangers had come up to the roof, two men and a woman. they had a walkie-talkie and wore uniforms. they walked past our water tank single-mindedly looking out over lohdalum bay. they were transmitting in english. you could hear them all over the roof. the messages from the naval ship spoke of a new wave.

we gathered around the uniformed people.

a new wave? when is it coming?

the uniformed men said nothing, but the woman said: in fifteen to twenty minutes.

how large is the wave? will the hotel withstand it?

we don't know, was the monotone answer we kept getting.

from somewhere out there a new wave was coming toward

us. we assumed that a warship had the appropriate technology to determine that. this hotel was built on sand. it could be washed away. why hadn't we gone up to the mountains with the group this afternoon? there we would surely have been safe. we'd had the chance to escape and botched it out of fear. the warship we thought we could just discern didn't come nearer. maybe it was waiting to see what would happen.

in the meantime everybody was awake, or had been awakened, the thai family camping beside us had begun to murmur prayers. elias, the first of our party to lie down and fall asleep from exhaustion, sat up straight. he said: the cigarettes are gone.

what cigarettes?

he pointed to the floor beside him. a carton of cigarettes was lying right here last night, someone must have taken it.

i said, a new wave may be coming. elias went out to the guard rail with me. edith, sophie, and emine stayed at our overnight spot.

we couldn't do anything but look out at the silver shimmering horizon, listen, and wait. now and then sophie came over to ask if we had learned anything more precise. we stood in a row at the edge of the flat roof for about half an hour. in the background, murmured prayers. sometimes a cry in the distance; sometimes the lapping waves of the sea. then the murmuring died down, and people began to talk to each other again. had they made a mistake? where on earth had the people in uniform gone? they had walked around on the flat roof with their walkie-talkies and then just disappeared.

i set about opening the bottle of blanc de blanc, but didn't have a corkscrew. the french had one, but i didn't want to ask them for anything more because, when we had left our place for a while toward evening, they had taken a couple of our blankets. i didn't want to go beg them for the blankets. they belonged to us as little as to them. but they had their whole backpacks and all we had were these blankets.

i wasn't able to force the cork down into the bottle, and

so i walked around among the solar panels, tanks, and pipes, with the bottle of blanc de blanc looking for an object that might serve to open this bottle. in the meantime, a strong stench emanated from the area of the solar panels, and it was advisable to move very cautiously around there. in the afternoon edith had walked over the whole flat roof with an american woman suggesting to people that they cut all empty bottles open and stand them up behind the solar collectors so that they could be used to urinate in. the row of tilted solar panels offered a bit of privacy in the brightly moonlit night, and made it a desirable place to use as a latrine. we five – emine had long since become one of us – had a small privilege compared to most of the others. we still had the roll of toilet paper that edith had taken from the room service cart. we guarded it under our blanket.

in this area of the solar collectors, which had become extraordinarily unappetizing, i was able to push the cork of the bottle of blanc de blanc all the way into the bottle with a pipe connector.

in the agitation over the new wave most people had started moving. they stood together in groups and conversed. the thais near us had stopped praying. the man groaned, the woman cried quietly to herself. their children seemed to have fallen back asleep.

we kept listening for the next wave as we passed the bottle of blanc de blanc around. what had we actually experienced? we didn't know. there was talk of an earthquake, and someone used the word tsunami. i knew that word. i had seen a bbc documentary about cumbre vieja, the active volcano nearly two thousand meter high on the canary island of la palma. a series of large earthquakes had followed its last eruption in 1949. after a week, the west side of the volcano had slid approximately four meters down to the sea. since then a fault crosses from north to south across the flank of the cumbre vieja.

in the documentary, two geologists from london made the

point that, in a new cumbre vieja eruption, its unstable west flank could break off and crash into the sea. the ensuing tsunami could strike the coast of west Africa first, then later submerge the west of england, and, finally, the american east coast. boston, new york, and miami wouldn't stand a chance.

a german geologist contradicted this theory. he considered it a horror scenario and claimed that any flooding of the american east coast was out of the question. the amount of stone that would slide into the sea during a volcanic eruption would be far smaller than what his british colleagues assumed.

the bbc documentary reported about yet another collapse of the side of a volcano which had taken place in 1959 in lituja bay in alaska. there, a rock mass over a thousand meters high had plunged into the water. the wave it caused towered a hundred and fifty meters high, crashed onto land, and surged another five hundred meters up the slopes. the documentary presented two witnesses to this event, who had been carried above the tree line in their boat.

i remembered this documentary vividly. it was interesting and suspenseful. i never thought that i would ever be affected by such a tidal wave. now i was talking about one. the men had spoken of an earthquake. i imagined that a part of a mountainside had slid into the sea on a neighboring island and thought the whole thing was probably a local geological event. we didn't have the slightest idea of the extent of the catastrophe. all communication lines with the outside world had broken down.

emine clung to edith like a little child. she asked how old our children were. she was surprised that we still took them along on vacation. then she told us that claude had two children about the same age. she said that claude was separated and this was her first vacation with him.

and then emine and edith talked about something not meant for my ears. i picked up a bit of it anyway, because sophie had to get involved. emine had gotten her period and didn't know what to do. sophie had spread out the contents of her backpack on the roof that afternoon, so it could dry. and some tampons had been among her things. a stroke of luck. i remember how grateful emine was when she got the tampons. she could hardly believe it. a tampon. what a luxurious gift.

27

a year after the tsunami, as i am packing my things to fly back to thailand with edith tomorrow morning, i suddenly feel a powerful anxiety. it occurs to me that i've chosen only black clothing. although i like to wear black, this choice suddenly seems like portent: we are flying to our deaths. i'd really prefer to unpack everything and cancel the trip. although my superstition feels ridiculous to me i still can't help unpacking a couple of black t-shirts and pants and substituting clothing of different colors. among these, some green shorts that come from thailand. but back then i didn't wear them, elias did.

during the night, or maybe it was in the evening, someone had brought a suitcase up to the roof of the phi phi hotel. i noticed this suitcase in the morning. it stood near our sleeping spot, and since it didn't belong to anyone, people went through it and took what they needed. it was made from blue and red canvas, had rollers on one side, and bore the logo roxy, the heart of surfing. i can report that precisely because the bag now stands in our storage closet in vienna.

during the afternoon, people broke into the rooms of those who hadn't returned. i watched that with unease. two men threw their whole body weight against a door until it opened. then they forced their way into a stranger's room and placed the belongings of the dead at everyone's disposal: the drinks in the minibar, the blankets and towels, toilet articles, clothing and shoes. but were the occupants of this room really dead? maybe they just hadn't made it back to the hotel yet and were safe somewhere else in a different building.

new rules applied: anyone who didn't stay with his

property relinquished his right to it. the survivors took whatever was to be had. a couple of men who had specialized in collecting beer cans and cigarettes drank and smoked all night on a terrace visible from our roof. that wouldn't have been possible on our roof. an american woman ran up to anyone who lit a cigarette and yelled, did he want to blow up the whole hotel? everything is broken around here, there could be a gas leak and the whole hotel would explode. normally the cigarette was put out immediately. but the american woman wasn't alert enough late at night. after we had finished the bottle of blanc de blanc, elias, i, and a german fellow all stood at the guard rail smoking cigarettes without disturbing anybody. the american woman had apparently fallen asleep.

the morning of december 27th started with the most wonderful noise, the landing of a helicopter. it brought nurses, first aid supplies, and a forester. the copter was loaded up with corpses and departed again. the sound of a chainsaw broke into the crippling silence that returned to the island after the beating of the rotor blades died away in the distance. as penetrating as the screaming of the motors was, it brought sighs of relief all around. finally something was happening.

emine and i left the roof of the phi phi hotel and went down to the first aid station. a man was cutting down palm trees. fantastic. that's going to make it easier for the helicopter to land. maybe even several could land. there seemed to be some prospect of getting away from here.

during the whole previous day ships large and small had appeared on the horizon again. they slowly approached the coast, and got up close to the carpet of debris. several made passages like ice breakers through the remains of civilization floating on the water. you could see people on board. the captains of the motor- and sailing yachts held binoculars and looked across at us from a safe distance. for a whole day we were objects of catastrophe-sightseeing. none of these ships came close enough to take anyone on board. it was as though we were lepers. the captains of the pleasure boats had presumably seen the film titanic and were now afraid that a struggle could break out for the precious spots on board.

we kept hearing rumors that a ship from the thai navy was on its way to us. but it was nowhere to be seen. and during the night, when we thought it was out there and we could see its outline, it brought no rescue, just misinformation about a new wave.

on the morning of december 27th the first aid station was expanded with additional mattresses from the cabana hotel. emine and i sat down on one of these mattresses and waited until a thai nurse found time to bandage our wounds. in the meantime we had developed a routine for handling the sandstorms that came up when the helicopter landed and took off: we wrapped the injured in sheets.

the helicopter had brought plastic bottles of drinking water. these were distributed at the helipad. emine and i took two bottles each and returned to the roof. there a woman announced in a loud, authoritative voice that the naval ship had finally come to our aid. we were all supposed to go down to the pier. up to this point edith had not left the roof. ever since some of our blankets had migrated over to the french-men, she had guarded our spot near the water tank. she had made sure that everybody had been able to keep a blanket and a towel to use as a pillow, and she hid the toilet paper from prying eyes. she also saw to it that we passed around the last bottle of water we had for the night equally, so that we five could each take a swallow. only now did she come downstairs for the first time.

we took the towels, put the toilet paper and water bottles in sophie's backpack, and began to make our way down. dead bodies were still lying on the mezzanine and in front of the reception area. someone had gathered them together and covered them over. on the way to the pier we passed other corpses, which lay uncovered. they were swollen and had developed brown and red spots. one man's scrotum was inflated like a balloon.

approximately two hundred people were gathered at the pier. we approached it hesitantly. in the midst of the wrecks of the speed boats, long-tail boats and other debris the green roofs of bungalows which once belonged to the cabana hotel stuck out of the water. they hadn't been crushed, just shoved into the sea. mostly diving instructors had lived in these bungalows. later i often encountered this image of the bungalows washed out into ton sai bay. it was used frequently in the reports about the tsunami.

we stood at the edge of the concrete pier, which had lost its guard-rail. a sweetish stench hung in the air. more corpses were laid out here on the beach of ton sai bay than on lohdalum bay. the second wave had carried them here. corpses were being transported on doors and set down on the beach beside the pier. family members wrapped their dead in sheets and bound them up in order to take them to the mainland. the sign decorated with four flags that read welcome to phi phi island hung there as though nothing had happened. debris rocked lazily on the water. there was no sign of any naval ship. then we heard screams, and panic broke out instantly. everybody began to run. we ran too, as fast as we could, across the wreckage and back to the entrance of the phi phi hotel. we didn't know what had happened. we thought a new wave was coming at us.

a quarter of an hour after leaving our spot on the roof, we found ourselves sitting beside the water tank on the roof of the phi phi hotel again. edith said she wasn't leaving this spot until she was sure we were really going to get away.

that lasted until around noon. then two ferry-boats actually appeared on the horizon of ton sai bay. they slowly picked their way through the debris up to the pier. people streamed toward them through the rubble. there were still a good four thousand people alive on the island. they all wanted to get away.

from the roof one could see that it was fruitless to try to snag a spot on one of the two ferries. we preferred to wait until more ships arrived. so we waited a while longer on the roof of the phi phi hotel, where bit by bit the crowd thinned out. bloodstains, empty bottles, torn clothing, towels, blankets, packing materials, bags, urine, and piles of excrement remained behind.

i was the only person in our family who wore a t-shirt and shorts. they had dried on my body the day before. edith, sophie and elias were in swimsuits. they protected themselves from the sun with sheets. the blue and red suitcase that had been looted several times still stood before us. i pulled it over and unpacked it. everything in it was still useful. when we were perched on the ledge, edith had taken off her torn top so i could wrap it around my hand. we found a blue sleeveless t-shirt for her in the suitcase, and there was a white tank-top for sophie. edith also found an eggshell-colored, cotton flounced skirt. it was much too big. so she tied it with a knot at her hip to keep it on. sophie got a pair of baggy black, knee-length wrap-around pants; elias got green shorts with cargo pockets labeled american eagle outfitters and a t-shirt. what's more, all of us got a little manicure set and a sampler packet from the body shop with 3 ml. vials of eau de toilette in different fragrances.

we packed our bath towels in the suitcase and left the flat roof of the phi phi hotel, where only the frenchmen were left, also getting ready to depart. among the things left behind was a book, an introduction to buddhism in english. elias took it. i also clearly remember the moment when i noticed an address tag hanging from the suitcase that i pulled behind me, lifting it over the pipes. just before we got to the staircase i glanced at the tag, tore it off, and dropped it on the floor. i didn't want to get caught with a stranger's suitcase.

it was obvious from its contents that the suitcase didn't belong to a slim young woman. from my quick glance at the tag all i gathered was that it had an american address. today i regret throwing that tag away. i hope the owner of this suitcase is still alive. i would gladly return her things to her with the deepest gratitude. we even saved the vials of eau de toilette with the fragrances chymara, citrella, amorito, altaro and minteva.

28

a year later, behind the cabana hotel, which is now a large construction site, there stands another, considerably smaller shell of a building. the french government and the french red cross, as banners in many languages announce, are financing the rebuilding of the hospital here. there is nothing left of the old infirmary. after the tsunami the island was left with no medical care whatsoever. the only medications and bandages available were those that the water had not swept away from a few private pharmacies.

we walk over to lohdalum bay, where, because it was low tide, the water has ebbed quite far out, just as when we arrived a year ago. only a few long-tail boats lie on the sand. a painted wooden sign that reads monkey bar points us to the end of the bay, behind which rises a steep, jungle-covered mountain. there, at the end of lohdalum bay, stands a hut, with improvised wooden scaffolding in front of it.

the owner, a man in his mid-thirties with a heavily tattooed bare torso, and two of his friends, are busy rebuilding the bar. at the moment it is just an open-air counter with a roof of palm fronds. a sign reads welcome, and another: fanta, sprite, soda, 30 baht. a carved wooden monkey sits on the bar.

there is only one other guest besides us, an englishman from southampton. ut, as the owner of the monkey bar is named, is glad that new customers have come. we tell him that our children were in this bar on the evening before the tsunami.

he says that nothing survived from the bar or his house. he had already been awake, because he had to run a few errands thanks to the christmas rush. he had just gone out when he saw the wave coming. he ran up the hill. both his brothers, one of them twenty, the other twenty-eight, were surprised in their sleep. he himself was evacuated to krabi the next day.

with the catamaran? i ask.

ut nods, and i say, we were probably on the same ship.

again and again, ut tells us, he came back from krabi to search for the spot where his hut and bar once stood. his brothers had disappeared without a trace, and nothing could be found of anything that had once belonged to him, absolutely nothing. it was as if the bar had never been there. then he and two friends decided to rebuild it. first the hut to live in. that's been finished in the meantime. now, the bar. to one side of the monkey bar, which gets its name from the monkeys that come down the mountain every morning to forage for food, ut has build a small wooden altar. there he places offerings in memory of his brothers and in the hope of a happier future.

the englishman from southampton has been listening to us. he was once a ship's cook and now dreams of settling down in southern spain and starting a family. actually he just wanted to pay a brief visit to this island, but now he's hung around here a couple of months. helping where he was needed.

while we talk, the bar owner's two friends are busy with saws, chisels, and planes. one of them says something about a bamboo pot. then he lights up a water pipe made of bamboo cane and lets us all have a few strong drags.

the other one also quits work on the bar. he prepares a fire for grilling. carrying two big fish and a few octopuses. ut walks a little way into the ocean to a flat spot where he begins to wash and gut the fish. i follow him and watch him work. he says that ideally he'd love to go fishing every day, but he lost his boat in the tsunami.

and this one here? i ask. we have just walked by a long-tail boat that lies on the beach right in front of the bar.

that doesn't belong to me, but i am allowed to use it, he says.

when we leave, ut gives us two hibiscus blossoms. we put these into a cut off plastic bottle in our bungalow.

we go out again in the evening to look for the second bar where our children had been on the night before the tsunami, the reggae bar. it's the largest bar on phi phi island. we are visiting it for the first time. by contrast to the monkey bar this place gets a lot of visitors. kids are mostly sitting around in the courtyard. the tables are grouped to form a boxing ring, where a kickboxing night is supposed to begin at ten p. m. loud reggae music is playing. large monitors broadcast uefa cup soccer games. two sides of this courtyard are surrounded by a three-story concrete building open at the front. on the second floor there are billiard and pool tables, on the top floor there is another bar and a dance floor.

the bar fills with kids from all over the world. people are drinking almost nothing but swedish buckets, which are on sale here. the deal is buy one bucket, get one free. the atmosphere is relaxed. two girls with low-cut tops come in. following them are two gentlemen dressed all in white whom they take to the bar and soon begin to kiss. edith and i observe the people. we begin to invent stories about them. even about the blonde who changes her hairdo four times during the course of the evening. in between, she leans her head close to her girlfriend's. they laugh and photograph themselves holding their camera at arm's length – until two gentlemen from the next table intervene helpfully and stay. not at ten, as announced, but rather at eleven o'clock the kickboxing begins. then one fight follows another. the crowd is wild and drunk.

this bar has every reason to celebrate. but i wonder whether the kids here are aware of it. anyone who made it here escaped hell. seventy percent of the houses all around were destroyed, but the reggae bar stayed standing and became the safe haven for hundreds of people from the surrounding streets.

we drink and watch the uninhibited partying, then the air

suddenly gets unpleasant, it starts to stink of sewage, and we leave right away. no matter where you sit on phi phi island, this can happen at any time. depending on how the wind blows. you can suddenly be overcome by a horrible stench because the tsunami completely destroyed the sewage system and it's still quite makeshift.

29

the rain just won't stop, so we have the big blue umbrella with the logo arayaburi resort with us. you can't walk a hundred meters in ton sai village without passing a massage parlor. massage! massage! the women call, and as they do so, they make the second a-sound long and let their voices rise a little. at the third or fourth parlor we decide to go in.

it looks just like a roomful of mattresses. we are not the only customers. it is funny to see how the petite thai women tackle the big european bodies. they climb right on top of them, take a seat, rub them down with oil, and roll their elbows all over them.

in front of me on a ledge there's a little shrine with a figure that seems to be both male and female. it holds up one hand like a greeting, but limp-wristed, as though it were making fun of gays. i imitate this gesture. the masseuse laughs. who is that? i ask. she says it is a zen buddha. a framed photo of a man stands next to the buddha.

when the masseuse begins to massage my left hand, she tries to pry my crippled little finger straight, but it doesn't work.

what's this? she asks.

my tsunami finger, i answer.

she laughs. i say, i really mean it. we begin to talk about the tsunami. the masseuse draws my attention to the photo next to the zen buddha and points to a female co-worker, who at that moment is giving a young blonde girl a manicure. that was her husband, she says. he died in the tsunami.

the widow is young, barely over twenty. she glances over to us. the masseuse lifts up my hand and explains to her colleague, in a voice that sounds as if she's telling a joke, how i got my crippled finger. the other woman, for her part, seems to be able to do nothing but laugh in response. her husband was a cook in the phi phi princess. but even as she says that, she still seems to be smiling.

how old was he? i ask.

twenty-three, she says, still smiling. only the blonde getting the manicure looks upset about it.

and you, i ask my masseuse, how did you survive?

she points to a stairway at the back end of the room. we all ran up there, she says. fortunately the house held up. she tells about the people on the street who died, of the neighbors, and keeps laughing the whole time. she says, she tried to get home as quickly as possible. all she could think of was getting home, but you know how long it took before anybody could leave.

instantly i recall the thais forcing their way to the pier, the tourists all screaming, calm down! stay in line! don't push! but that didn't help. the thais saw the ship at anchor. they screamed in confusion; they limped and slid between us with their packs and bags and couldn't be stopped. we got out of their way because we were afraid of being shoved into the water.

the pier was a shaky concrete platform. the side sections that had supported the guard rail had been torn away by the wave. we were afraid that the platform might collapse under the weight of the crowding mass of people. although the thais were otherwise so helpful, there was no stopping them once the first ships arrived. they wanted to escape this island as fast as possible and get home to their families. the first ships to leave phi phi island were dangerously overloaded. even while the gangplank was being pulled onboard some people jumped across onto the ship and clung to the railing.

the masseuse says she cried so much, more than in her whole life. she couldn't earn any money for a whole half year. she talks about crying and laughs as she does it. later, when she is almost finished with the massage, she asks me which full moon party i'm going to tonight. i don't know anything about a full moon party. she explains that tonight everyone will be having full moon parties. i say i'm probably going to stay home. she gestures toward edith, who is being massaged a couple of mattresses away in the same room, and asks, with the wife? i say yes. she says: and when the wife is asleep, then you come to our full moon party.

when we pay and edith has already gone outside, she leans over to me slightly and whispers into my ear: i want to see you tonight.

we go to a restaurant opposite the massage parlor. it has been redecorated with elegant dark wood furniture. here, according to a brochure, one can take courses in thai cooking. there is a bookcase by our table with an english guidebook to thailand lying on it. it was published before the tsunami. the part about the phi phi islands has been consulted so often that the book falls open to the place. there you can read about the burgeoning tourist industry and get a precise description of all the hotels and lodgings. and then there is also a report about a distant village on the north side of the island that is apparently inhabited by nomadic seafarers, the so-called sea gypsies. there's no tourism there.

the restaurant owner is an englishman, he serves us the thai dishes on square porcelain plates. during the tsunami he was working in phuket in another restaurant, which was spared. i ask him about the sea gypsies. he says not one of them died. when the sea retreated at the wrong time for the leeward tide, they fled to the mountains.

after our meal i watch a pencil-thin rastafarian guy in the shop next door piercing the nipple of a tourist to the sound of loud heavy metal music. first everything is laid out on a tray, disinfectant, a thick needle, sterile gauze, tweezers, q-tips, and vaseline. the steel nipple ring that the customer has chosen is placed into a disinfecting liquid, the freshly unpacked needle stuck into the vaseline. the young man lies down on a chaise longue like an operating table. the rastafarian pulls down a light and turns it on. this illuminates the customer's left breast. heavy-metal music keeps thudding in the background. the rastafarian tears open a plastic package, takes out antiseptic gloves and puts them on. two of the customer's friends take up positions where they can see him well and turn on their video cameras. the customer's left breast is disinfected, then the nipple is grasped with the tweezers and punctured with the needle. the young man tenses his mouth somewhat. the steel ring is inserted into the eye at the back end of the needle, which is pulled through, and the ring sticks in the nipple. it just has to be screwed shut. the procedure is almost bloodless.

30

we are taking a boat ride out to sea. it happens to be the first day since our return to phi phi island that the sun shines without interruption. a hundred people could have found places on this ship, but because of the constant rain during the past week only about twenty people have signed up for the all-day tour. the young man in charge of us counts the vegetarians on board for lunch and distributes diving masks, snorkels, and fins. before the tsunami, he tells me, he used to live with his mother in a neighborhood of huts in the middle of ton sai village. he just happened to be on board a ship where the passengers were getting ready for a dive. suddenly the sea turned murky, and an unusually strong current developed. too strong to go diving. so they turned back and didn't find anyplace to moor the boat. his mother's corpse wasn't found until weeks later, when they were shoveling away the debris.

during the morning we sail around phi phi leh and snorkel in the midst of hundreds of other tourists. beneath us the gleaming colors of the reefs, above us the steep cliffs. on deck edith and i have seats beside two young scottish girls who have been travelling for three months, mostly in the rain, as they say. they are so excited by today's sunshine that it takes them until noon, when we return to phi phi don, to notice how red their skin has gotten.

our boat anchors in the outer area of ton sai bay, on long beach, which is a favorite among young tourists because lodgings are cheaper here than in ton sai village. a long-tail boat brings a shipment with box lunches, which are handed across to our boat. our thai tour leader passes the styrofoam containers around. meat or vegetarian? he asks.

they are the exactly same type of styrofoam containers that they unloaded from the helicopter on december 27, 2004, and they contain the same food: rice with chicken or rice with vegetables.

we had waited a couple of hours in the area of the makeshift first aid station near the helipad because we were hoping the crowds at the pier would thin out. meanwhile we all had bandages on hands and feet. edith had some on her back, too, and emine, on her chest. we sat on the ground or, whenever there was a spot free, on one of the mattresses. we drank water, which a helicopter had delivered that morning. we walked around and inspected the disaster a little more closely. we were waiting for the crowd at the pier to thin out. but we still had a long time to wait. since the first ships had begun to arrive, more and more people gathered. many were being carried. and then a helicopter came, from which hundreds of styrofoam containers were unloaded. we sat on the ground and ate this rice dish. not counting the few crackers that we had gotten the night before, this was our first meal after the tsunami. but nobody had much appetite in the middle of this ruined landscape, and the smell of putrefaction became stronger with each hour.

elias remembers that he went over to the cabana hotel to use the toilet. he entered one of the destroyed corridors, which was full of debris and wreckage, because in the cabana the wave had positively exploded through the ground floor. coming toward him he saw a guy with an axe. familiar with recent horror films, elias feared the worst. in his own words: i thought he had gone crazy because of the wave. he's coming for me. i get really scared. he gives me a friendly smile, takes a passport out of his pocket and asks me if i recognize it. i was relieved but i couldn't help him. he was looking for his brother. then he broke down a door with the axe and i kept going, still looking for a toilet. then i went into one of the rooms that was standing open. there was a boat inside. it had been pushed inside right over the terrace. the toilet was already completely filled with shit. i left the door open because there wasn't any light, still scared that somebody might catch me because i was in somebody else's room using the bathroom. i think i was already kind of crazy myself.

once we got through all this throng and finally found ourselves on the motorized catamaran again that afternoon, we didn't know where the boat was headed. the main thing was to get away from the island, away from the dead. once on board we discovered we were on a ferry to krabi. the captain cast off after all passengers who had jumped on deck after the official boarding had left the ship again. that was reassuring. we had a captain who wasn't willing to expose us to any new danger.

once we reached krabi we encountered an almost overwhelming eagerness to help. a first aid station had been set up at the boat landing. all the injured were examined here and given new bandages. in addition to some minor injuries, sophie had a deep cut on her foot. she cooperated while her wound was being dressed. we were just being treated at the moment and weren't able to come to her aid, but we just noticed that she suddenly became very pale and collapsed. the nurse held a little vial of something under her nose.

in sophie's words: the little vial contained ammoniac. i was pretty much out of it. suddenly i felt two hands grabbing my face from behind. they took hold of my temples and my forehead and began to massage me. gradually i could see straight. it wasn't the nurse, but an old woman who was massaging me. a thai. her clothing consisted of some rags thrown over her, and to me she looked a little like a sorceress. her movements were very gentle and slow. that helped. she undid my braid and began to comb through my hair with her fingers. she also massaged my scalp. then she dug into her pocket and pulled out two purple hair clips decorated with sparkling stones. she separated my hair into two braids and attached these to the back of my head with the clips, so my hair wasn't hanging down into my face in this heat. it was incredible that in the middle of such a huge disaster somebody thought to give me such a beautiful hairdo. it was a loving gesture, which helped to relax some of the stress i felt. i don't know how long i lay there, with my head on the old woman's lap, but i think it was a pretty long time. when i finally got up, she pressed a colorful little stick into my hand, which looked like a pencil. there was a liquid in it. she told me to spray this liquid into my nose and breathe in. she kept smiling the whole time. she had such a sincere and calming smile.

i observed sophie's encounter with the old woman out of the corner of my eye, because just then my injuries were being washed out with disinfectants, which wasn't exactly pain free. a doctor decided that i had to be taken to a hospital. they shipped me over into a waiting ambulance where other injured people were already sitting. i insisted that my family had to come too. but there wasn't room in the truck for all of us, so i got out again. while waiting for the next ambulance, we didn't want to block the few spaces in the first aid station, which were needed for other injured people, so we left the landing. behind the coastal road there was a row of little snack shops and kiosks with roofed-over seating areas. we flopped down there. the woman to whom the kiosk belonged greeted us as if we might be customers. when she saw that we couldn't buy anything, because we had no money, she led us to the cooler and let each of us choose a drink. there were still five of us. as a twenty-eight-year-old, emine could have been our daughter. edith and i had been married for exactly that many years.

but then we were separated from emine. when the next ambulance arrived, once again there wasn't enough space for all of us, because naturally the injured took precedence. then a doctor spoke to a private citizen and requested that he take us to the hospital. but just the family, he said. the other woman has to stay here. she's going to be taken to a collection point by bus. emine didn't want to be separated from us.

she speaks only french, i said. the doctor asked among the other volunteer helpers working in the first aid station to find out if anyone spoke french. a young canadian woman raised her hand. she said she would look after emine. the man who was supposed to take us to the hospital was already waiting. the canadian woman took emine by the arm and wanted to take her away from the first aid station. we just had time to hug her goodbye and wish her well. but because none of us had anything to write with we couldn't exchange addresses or telephone numbers in all this rush. emine had tears in her eyes when we turned away from her and went to his car with the thai man.

since then we've often spoken of this bitter parting. but at the time we were in no position to contradict the doctor's orders.

at the hospital in krabi we drove up to patients lying outdoors on beds and gurneys because inside, the hospital was already completely overcrowded. nonetheless an astonishingly well-functioning emergency system was already in place. the entrance hall was a mass operating room. to the left of the entrance there was a busy reception team. they diagnosed and registered every patient who arrived. the bandages that had just been put on me an hour earlier were removed again, and they attached a tag to my arm. on it stood the date of admission: 12-27-2547. in order to calculate the date by our calendar, one has to subtract five hundred and forty-three years, because according to buddhist tradition, buddha attained nirvana at the age of eighty, five hundred and forty-three years before christ. after that, my name, my age, country of origin, and then the name of the triage doctor, peter. following this the diagnosis was written in thai. i was shown to a bed in the entrance hall that had just become free. there i lay down and waited a quarter of an hour. then one of the many three-person teams came up to me with a medical cart. a woman doctor, a woman nurse, and a male nurse. they got right to work. i let them do anything they wanted. my only concern was that they use a sterile syringe. the nurse who had bandaged me that morning on phi phi island recommended that i pay attention to that. the male nurse took a syringe sealed in plastic from the medical cart. the woman doctor – today i doubt whether she really was a trained doctor – anaesthetized my little finger and ring finger with several injections, and then sutured the wounds. she found two more cuts on my middle finger. i don't know whether it was because she didn't have enough local anaesthetic anymore, but, at any rate, the doctor said that now it was going to hurt a little – it would be best if i pressed my feet against the bottom of the bed. the nurses held my hand. the doctor sutured both cuts on my middle finger. i tried to hold my hand as still as possible, while my feet pushed against the bed so hard that my back arched.

before the hand could be bandaged i had to wait for a supervising physician. she was going from bed to bed examining all patients who were supposed to be discharged. a young man, maybe a volunteer, accompanied her carrying a folder and a stamp pad. the supervising physician was filling out discharge forms with carbon copies. whenever the supervising physician examined a patient, the young man ran to the reception team at the entrance to deliver the carbon copy of the previous patient. there the data were entered into a computer.

the supervising physician examined my fingers, which had been sewn together. then she said something in thai. she pointed to the sutures. the woman who had treated me, took a scalpel in her hand, and finger by finger, opened all the sutures. with a pair of tweezers, the nurse removed all the stitches and laid them on a tray that the male nurse held for her. the supervising physician explained to me in english that the wounds were infected and had to be kept open. then she separated the flesh on my little finger and said – which i had already comprehended when i was sitting on the ledge of the phi phi hotel – that the ligaments had been severed and needed a separate operation.

i left the krabi hospital in the same condition that i entered it. nonetheless, i am grateful to this hospital for three essential acts of kindness. while i was being treated, edith was permitted to telephone our family in austria. i received two little plastic bags for the journey. one contained painkillers, the other a strong antibiotic. and i received my discharge form, which stated very clearly: urgently needs hospital treatment. one day later this form was very useful in helping the austrian embassy employee in bangkok make a good argument when he tried to persuade austrian airlines to take us to vienna.

31

it's mid-january, 2005, and i am lying in the lorenz-böhler hospital in vienna. they have cut open the entire length of my little finger and sutured together the shrunken ligaments where they were severed. because of the bad infection the operation had to wait for two weeks after our arrival in vienna.

now and then a man in a wheelchair emerges from the room across the way. he may be about forty years old, unshaven, with short graying hair. this morning the minister of defense paid him a visit. when the man in the wheelchair travels along the corridor after eating, i later find him in the stairwell, drinking coffee from a dispensing machine and smoking a cigarette. we start a conversation.

the man is named johann baumgartner and comes from tyrol. he was in khao lak with his wife regina and his son david. his wife is in the intensive care unit on the floor below, his eleven-year-old son is among the missing. johann baumgartner says, there are indications that david is still alive. as soon as he gets out, he plans to travel to thailand to look for him.

they were in their bungalow. david was sitting at the open entrance with his feet on the terrace. suddenly a loud roaring, rushing sound could be heard. the wooden bungalow tipped to the side and water poured through the door. johann baumgartner assessed the situation. quickly, into the bathroom, he yelled. the bathroom was the only room in the bungalow with masonry walls. they ran into the bathroom. but within seconds the wave came. the walls shook, the tiles came off.

then the whole bungalow collapsed, and the water carried them away.

johann baumgartner tells this in a calm and composed manner. i ask him for a cigarette.

he was underwater a long time and had actually given up hope. then he managed to get to the surface through the debris and stay afloat in the carpet of wreckage that was moving inland. he was deposited, with everything else around him, on the edge of the national park. he freed himself from the wreckage and ran into the mountains with others. he had deep wounds on his legs and was taken to a hospital. two days later he learned that his wife was in the hospital in phuket, alive but badly injured.

ever since then his large family has been busy trying to find david by telephone and internet. there are many thais who confirm having seen him. primarily, there's an entry in one of the smaller hospitals that says that a david baumgärtner was treated for two days. the umlaut must surely be a typo. since then all attempts to trace him have failed, but the clues have increased. a dowser offered his services in the search. johann was skeptical of this method of searching, but, given the situation, grateful for any help. he tells me, as soon as he gets out of here, nothing is going to keep him in vienna. he is going to find his son.

johann baumgartner passes the open door of my hospital room in his wheelchair a couple of hours later. he pauses briefly and reports that his wife is better. he has to take her some homeopathic medications.

in the evening, which in hospitals begins very early and can last a long time, my two roommates are busy with their television sets. in order to read in peace, i go out into the hall and sit down in one of the visitors' armchairs.

there's something strange about the book i'm reading at the moment, john irving's hotel new hampshire. i met john irving at a reading in iowa, where he read from his then latest novel, son of a circus. the next day i bought several books by him. on the return flight to vienna i began to read hotel new hampshire, but for years never got to finish it. before we left for phi phi island i pulled this book off the shelf and began to read it again on the flight to bangkok. it disappeared in the deluge with all our things. a week later in vienna, while i was focused on finding my way back into normal life, one of my errands was to pick up a package that had been held for us at the post office in our absence. the package contained the latest volume in the series of novels published by the süddeutsche zeitung, john irving's hotel new hampshire. i took it to the hospital with me and now continued reading in german the text that i had begun in english.

but then i am distracted. an old woman with a white head bandage is being pushed along the corridor in her bed. the bed is left in front of the glass window of the office of the nursing station. the woman begins to rattle the raised bed rails. then she sits up and keeps repeating, i'm cold, i'm cold ...

a nurse comes, lays her down and covers her over. the
woman goes on: i'm cold, i'm cold, i'm cold ...

the nurse goes into a patient's room. the woman with the
head bandage sits up again. she looks across at me. i have given
birth to three children, she says. then she says: help me. why
won't anybody help me? help! who will help me?

she gets louder and louder. the nurse returns.

why does it hurt so much? asks the old woman.

because your skin is torn off, says the nurse. it's best if you
lay your hand like this, just leave the hand there, and in a half-
hour we'll look at it again.

the nurse goes back into the patient's room. a male nurse
approaches the old woman. he says: good evening, my name is
thomas and this evening i have the night shift with nurse silvia.

the old woman asks: where am i here?

you're in the hospital, you're out in the hallway.

i've given birth to three children.

don't get up, stay lying down.

i have to go to the toilet.

come, i'll help you. don't hold on there hold onto me.

is the toilet so far away?

no, it's right here. come, let's go.

during all this another old woman is wheeled out to the
nurses' station in her bed. she too begins to rattle the raised
bed rails.

hello, who's there? she calls, when she sees me.

the male nurse brings the woman with the head bandage
back and leaves.

the woman with the head bandage asks the other woman,
is there a toilet here? the other doesn't know.

if only it weren't so far, says the woman with the head
bandage, i know the toilet is really far away.

very far, says the other one.

the woman with the head bandage sits up and is about to
stand up, when the male nurse comes and lays her down again.

we were just at the toilet, he says.

but i have to make pee pee, says the woman.

hello from alzheimer's, says the male nurse. he gets a wheelchair and takes the woman to the toilet again. in the meantime, the other one sits up.

which is the way to the toilet? she asks, and begins to shake the bed rails. she nurse comes out of a patient's room. she helps her out of bed and accompanies her to the toilet. once both women are lying in bed again, they get sippy cups with tea from the nurse. then the nurse goes away.

and where is the toilet? asks the woman with the head bandage. she sits up. she begins to yell, i have to go to the toilet. i have to go to the toilet.

the male nurse comes. he says: i can't be taking you to the toilet every two minutes. do you go this often at home?

yes, is the clear answer.

i'll bring you the bedpan, says the male nurse, and leaves.

the woman with the head bandage asks the other one: where is the toilet around here?

i don't know. you know what? just say, i'll do it in the bed! say it out loud, i'm going to do it in bed!!

but instead the woman with the head bandages just keeps saying: i have to go to the toilet. have to go to the toilet. she is taken to the toilet again by the male nurse.

she is barely back in bed again when he is called back, this time by the other woman. she says: this woman wants to know something.

what does she want to know?

she wants to know where the toilet is.

no, says the male nurse, don't do this to me.

then i'm just going to pee on myself, says the woman with the head bandage.

and as the male nurse leaves, she continues: i'm just an ordinary patient. you never find out where the toilet is.

i have to write this down, i think, and go back to my room. i boot up the laptop, which helmut, a journalist friend, has lent me to substitute for the one the tsunami swallowed, and with

my right index finger i type the scene i have just experienced.
all in lower case. i'm still under the illusion that the little finger
of the left hand will be the one controlling the shift key once it
is freed from the splint and moving again. at this time i don't
yet know that the unsatisfactory healing process will encourage
me to make my own modest personal contribution to german
spelling reform.

edith visits me the next morning. she tells me what she
dreamed during the night. she says they laid her in a coffin. she
simply accepted it. the coffin wasn't even narrow. she had
plenty of room in it and could look out through a little
window. next to her there stood another coffin, in which
another woman was also lying. that woman had begun to
struggle for air. the gasping was getting louder and louder. it
was clear that the woman next to her was suffocating. suddenly
edith realized that she was going to suffocate too. when she
couldn't breathe anymore, she woke up in deadly panic.

after my hospital stay i go to physical therapy every day.
first in vienna and, as soon as i begin working at the university
again, in leipzig too. at one of my first physical therapy
sessions in the lorenz-böhler hospital, i happen to run into mr.
baumgartner. now he can get around on crutches without a
wheelchair. he is on his way to his wife, who is still in intensive
care. he beams at me. for the first time the doctors have given
him real hope that she's going to make it. he doesn't know
anything new about his son david. all of his relatives are still
researching by internet. they are also planning a trip to
thailand.

five months later, on june 20, i read about family members
of austrian tsunami victims in an article in the magazine profil.
in it there is a report on the funeral of david baumgartner, an
eleven-year-old pupil from the franciscan gymnasium in hall in
tyrol. several family members and friends had traveled to
thailand to search for david. they returned to austria without

any result. it wasn't until april 4th that his body could be identified by his t-shirt, his watch, and his trousers. confirmation by forensic investigation followed later. david was buried in his home village of taur.

32

after the tsunami international volunteers were working in the area in front of the hospital in krabi, amidst a strange confusion of cars and sick beds. they carried signs that designated which languages they could communicate in. when i left the hospital edith had already telephoned her father, and sophie, a girlfriend, whom she couldn't reach. elias didn't want to talk to anyone.

the three of them were standing with a volunteer from australia, who suggested that we go to the maritime hotel. she told us that a collection point for refugees had been set up there. in her eyes we were refugees, displaced persons. we were told that refugees were being registered in the maritime hotel and that we could find embassy employees there. how do we get there? we asked. she said, it's too far on foot, we should take a taxi. but we had no money. so she gave us five hundred baht, around ten euros, which was very generous for a taxi ride in thailand. she sent us across the square, where several group taxis were parked alongside the hospital wall.

the rear door of the first taxi, a minibus, stood open. several people were already sitting inside, among them a woman with her leg in a splint and crutches. we gave the driver the name of the maritime hotel, and he waved us in. clearly all the foreigners who came from the hospital were being transferred in these group taxis. once the minibus was full and people were already getting into the next one, the driver stood outside a while and had a discussion with a uniformed man, who had come from the hospital. we were not able to gather that in this conversation they had established a new destination for us. the driver tried to explain something to us as he drove off, but we didn't understand him, he didn't speak any foreign language.

in a crowded street he halted in front of an optician's. a young couple got out and came back after a while. they thanked him warmly, the woman was carrying a new pair of reading glasses. apparently this brief stop had been agreed upon before the trip. then we proceeded out of town, to our surprise. maybe, we thought, this maritime hotel wasn't in the city, but somewhere outside, on the beach. but we never caught a glimpse of the coast. we drove through a landscape of steep, thickly overgrown hilltops that resembled enormous cones. some were so similar in form they almost looked artificial. at the foot of a steep hill, our taxi drove through an archway and stopped on a gravel path.

instead of a hotel the only thing visible here was a buddhist temple with a chedi, a high bell-shaped tower, and around it a couple of stands selling drinks and devotional items. we let the others get out but we stayed in the car ourselves. the woman with her leg in a splint was probably using crutches for the first time in her life, because she was very unsteady when she walked. she also had a backpack, which someone carried for her. when the driver came back we said: maritime hotel, but he just shook his head and gestured to us to get out too. then he drove away. we were stranded in a wat, a buddhist temple and monastery complex.

a man wearing a traditional orange monk's robe greeted us with folded hands and led us through a dining room with rough-hewn wooden tables to a flight of steps. the woman with the crutches couldn't make it up these stairs, she had to be carried. we came to a second chamber, which was right over the dining room. the room was a good hundred square meters large and around four meters high. from the ceiling there hung two rows of five fans each, set on high speed. they whooshed and wobbled and produced a strong breeze. the room was completely bare. there were several compartments built into the front wall, in which there lay raffia mats. the monk gestured to us that we should each take one of these mats. and then we separated.

we four settled down on the long side of the chamber under a window. i chose the spot because it lay exactly between two fans, so it wasn't quite as breezy here. we lay our mats beside each other on the floor and on top of these the towels from the phi phi hotel, and what's more in precisely the order in which we had been lying on the flat roof. elias, me, sophie, and edith. of course on the hotel roof emine had had her sleeping place right beside edith. the next night was confirmed, and that was a comforting feeling.

in addition to us there were six other people in this chamber. the woman with the splinted leg had settled down a little distance from us, but on the same side. she took a book out of her backpack, but most of the time just stared straight ahead without reading in the book. i asked her if there were anything i could do for her. she said no and did not seem to be interested in conversation with me. i discovered eventually that she came from england and had been travelling with a woman friend. the friend was dead.

later she had a visitor. a woman spoke quietly to her. i did not understand what she said, but it sounded like a talk therapy session. the injured englishwoman said almost nothing herself. she seemed almost to be in a trance. we observed her and felt better that someone had come to look after her. otherwise, she would have been the only person in the room who had no one.

on the opposite side, on the other long wall, the couple that had gotten out at the optician's were laying out their mats, and next to them was a family with a child about four years old. we thought that from now on taxi after taxi would come and bring more people, but that was not the case. we remained the only ones in this large hall.

now and again one of the bald monks came by, smiling cordially, to place a bowl of rice at our feet. i wanted to phone the austrian embassy, to enquire what official advice they could give us about our situation, but the monk said they had no telephone here. we were to rest. he could probably smell our physical condition, because he led us back to the steps and from there to a small nearby room with a simple shower. edith was absolutely ecstatic. she jumped right in.

in the shower's anteroom there lay a washbasin with a piece of soap. we used it to wash ourselves and clean our clothing. but we had to go about our work with a certain frugality because there was just this small piece of soap, which was probably meant for all the others too. we had to help each other wash our bodies because we were all bandaged on our arms and legs. we hung out our things to dry on the window and set about trying to find out where on earth we were.

our first expedition into the monastery complex soon came to an end. we were wearing swimsuits. even though the monks and nuns – there were also women in this wat – said nothing, we didn't feel comfortable in bikinis and bathing trunks in the middle of a buddhist temple complex. so we went back and put on our wet t-shirts and shorts.

i also put the five hundred baht that we had gotten from the australian volunteer into my pocket. the taxi driver hadn't asked for money. he had either decided to waive the fare or been paid by the other passengers. we had been left sitting in the taxi and just hadn't noticed. now that we could have a look at the place with greater tranquility, it became apparent that everything was actually pretty decayed. the highest of the sharply pointed towers, the chedi, was the only one that had been restored recently. all the other temple buildings had more or less faded, or were crumbling away. there was a sign inviting contributions to save this important temple complex.

a moped driver came through the archway into the wat. he parked his vehicle beside some steps carved into the cliff and took a small bag from his luggage rack. he greeted us with folded hands. we asked him whether there were a shop nearby where we could purchase groceries and toothbrushes. there was a shop here in the wat, he said, but it was really very small.

at this hour it should still be open.

he was, as he explained, a lay brother, who lived high up on the mountain in a solitary hut. we asked him how far he had to climb. one hour, he said, but sometimes it took an hour and a half. he told us that he came down early every morning and drove into town to beg, and climbed back up every evening. then he showed us the way to the shop and began to ascend the knee-high steps, which went past another temple, carved right into the cliff. we watched him until he disappeared behind a bend in the path.

we found the shop and bought toothbrushes, toothpaste, a bar of soap, a comb, and a large bottle of water. we also looked for sunscreen, but didn't find any, and probably wouldn't have had enough money for it. when we did have a little money left over, i made a gesture of rubbing my skin to the old man behind the counter. in response he brought out a little bottle of oil.

we felt better after making these purchases. step by step we were winning back our normalcy. we could wash and brush our teeth again, anoint our raw skin, fix our hair, and had plenty of water. we took our new treasures back to our sleeping quarters. in the meantime, someone had delivered a pile of styrofoam packets to us, with the same rice dishes we had gotten on phi phi island. we shared two packages among us. elias said: this tastes rotten, i can't eat it.

the taste of the rice dish combined in his memory with the smell of decay on phi phi island, which was only a half day ago. he managed to swallow just a few bites.

33

the first days after our return are filled with minutiae, and that's the way it should be. we need to get new passports, new drivers' licenses, bank cards, credit cards, a rail pass for the german railway, a frequent user card for the austrian railway, i.d. cards for the streetcar systems in vienna and leipzig, a new inspection certificate for the car, new cell phones, new house keys, new membership cards for various organizations. that keeps us on the go. every day we discover new things we're missing. no glasses, no shaver, the disappeared laptop. our names have to be removed from various missing persons lists where our relatives put them. hospital appointments, eye doctor, official business, constant phone calls from journalists. in the meantime our story has been carried in the austrian media, and so all the phone calls from colleagues, from robert schindel, michael scharang, marie-thérèse kerschbaumer, barbara neuwirth, doron rabinovici, all asking how i'm doing – which make me happy.

on january 30th, when i can finally access my email, i realize that not only our family knew that we had gone to thailand, but others too, like friends from leipzig who have no contact with my family or with edith's. i read their worried emails, which they sent over and over to all the email addresses that we use. once i have my cell phone again and reinstate my connection, the text messages written after december 26th drift in. it takes me a while to inform people that we're still alive.

but that is, as i said, the way it should be. it keeps us on the move, prevents us from peering into this black hole, which is opening beneath us without our noticing. but at night we can't escape it.

elias dreams that he is walking down to the courtyard to empty the garbage. there lies his father, dead, near the dumpster. he takes me on his shoulders and, with great effort, carries me up four flights of stairs to our apartment. he can barely manage, but he won't give up. once he gets upstairs, he wakes up.

sophie's face changes. she gets a severe case of neurodermatitis. she thought she had gotten over this condition long ago. in order to earn a little pocket money on the side sophie has worked part-time as a model for a few years. now she has several job offers, but can't accept any. she rubs loads of cortisone onto her face, but as soon as she stops, her skin breaks out again.

i inform both school principals that elias and sophie have gone through the tsunami and its consequences, and i ask them to tell my children's teachers about their possible traumatization. elias's first school day starts with math class. he tells his teacher that unfortunately, he had taken his math notebooks to thailand, where they got lost in the deluge.

never mind, she answers, nobody could read your handwriting anyway.

later, at the end of the class, she asks him how he's doing. elias answers, not well. in response, the teacher says: it's probably best if you focus hard on math, then you'll forget quickly.

we know nothing of this conversation, we just notice that something is wrong.

elias comes home and says, he can't handle the school day, he doesn't want to go to school anymore.

and what do you want to do? edith asks.

he doesn't know. we try to persuade him not to give up now, just before graduation. then he starts to cry and we see that he is completely despondent. he lies down in bed. his friend paul has given him his math notebooks to copy, but elias doesn't get up until long after the copy shop has closed. he can't cope with this quick pace of constantly getting things done and catching up. he wants us to stay near him. he doesn't want to be alone in the apartment.

sophie dreams that the water has reached vienna. she is running home from the drasche park with her friend marianne, pursued by the water. they race up the stairs, but the water rises just as fast, story by story. whenever they turn around it's right behind them. once they are at our apartment on the fifth floor the water keeps rising and they run farther up the stairway to the attic. suddenly the attic turns into our apartment in leipzig. they step out onto the terrace and feverishly talk about where they can get hold of a boat in order to escape. they can't solve the problem. the water sloshes over the terrace, and she wakes up.

in all her dreams, she's trying to escape.

the dream about the coffin won't let go of edith. she dreams it over and over in new variations. then another dream follows it, in which a teacher colleague of hers has died and she has to visit the husband and daughters to console them, but the husband and daughters are amazingly calm. she desperately tries to explain the situation. but the death of the mother doesn't interest the children at all. it leaves the husband cold too.

i'm the only one who doesn't have any nightmares at first. but during the day i sometimes find myself reacting oddly. while walking along the ringstrasse in vienna to get a new membership card from the drivers' club, i hear a scream behind me. i automatically look around to find an entryway to run into and a stairway to escape on. just as i begin to run toward the hotel bristol, i realize the absurdity of my behavior. there's not going to be a wave here. i try to identify the source of the noise. there's a farmers' demonstration on schwarzenbergplatz.

we are often asked about our experiences and we talk about them as best we can. i'm more talkative than the others. elias knows many details, but he lacks a coherent context for the memories. sophie also has major gaps in her memories. edith vividly re-experiences the time when she felt sure she was going to die and one evening she just breaks down crying. we speak about our situation a lot, about our dreams and anxieties, but we are ultimately overwhelmed. three weeks after the tsunami we see no way out and seek professional help. i am present only at the first session. edith, sophie and elias are prescribed antidepressants. in addition the children receive a course of therapy. sophie turns to a specialist, who makes the connection with her neurodermatitis and, as it turns out, treats it effectively.

elias's dreams become more elaborate, but the threatening stories end better. they still often involve death. around two weeks after the therapy begins, he dreams that i am taking a cigarette out of a pack in the kitchen. he offers me a light, and suddenly my whole body bursts into flames like tinder. he can't stop it and watches me sink to the floor. i'm not incinerated, but i am dead. sophie comes and gives advice. she wraps my corpse in our blue kitchen rug. soon afterwards elias returns to the kitchen for a look. he opens the rug, touches me gingerly, notices that my body is still warm. he decides to try mouth to mouth resuscitation. i start coughing and vomiting violently, but i'm alive again.

when he tells me this, i heave a sigh of relief. i take it as a good sign that i am allowed to live again in his dreams. i still feel bad because i lost sight of him completely during the catastrophe. i don't know where he was when the wave came. nor does he seem to know for sure.

where was he swallowed by the wave? where was he spat out again? where did he save the child? where did a girl his own age grab hold of him and pull him under again? i didn't pick up any of those details; and a year later i am going to try to reconstruct them.

in mid-february i go to a lecture in vienna's kreisky forum. afterward, a jewish friend of mine, joanna, comes up to me. she sees my splinted, bandaged hand, and asks whether i've had a skiing accident. i say no, that was the tsunami. she is a bit shocked and obviously has the feeling that she doesn't want to let other topics overshadow my tsunami experience. there is an awkward moment. she knows how to deal with it by telling me about a friend of an israeli friend of hers who was on an indian island where the tsunami killed a couple of people and caused considerable damage, but where nobody had any idea of the extent of the whole catastrophe. there was no electricity and no contact to the rest of the world. the people on this island thought the wave was a local phenomenon. that's why her friend's friend didn't see any reason to leave the island or phone home. he was busy helping the locals and meant to keep doing that until his vacation was over. it wasn't until a week later when indian patrol boats arrived with aid that the inhabitants learned the extent of the disaster. then he phoned home. for a whole week his family and friends had tried in vain to find out if he were still alive. they had given up thinking he had survived.

a good six months after the tsunami, kurt neumann, head of vienna's literary forum alte schmiede, asks me to write a text for an anthology. all i can think of is thailand. nothing occurs that isn't related to the tsunami. and so i actually begin to write about it. i approach the story from the end. i tell how it was when we got the contents of our room safe back from thailand. and suddenly it seems to me – the man who thought he had the greatest perspective on all of this – that it's all oppressively close. only now do my nightmares begin. they continue night after night. sometimes they're very clear, sometimes just vague, but i still wake up bathed in sweat. i put work on the manuscript aside for a while and, because i have at least begun it, i can now turn to other topics. my request that sophie and elias tell me their tsunami memories once again triggers nightmares in them. as before, these have to do with water. but the dreams have become less threatening, and always end well.

elias dreams he is walking through the city with me. we

encounter a puddle of muck. it isn't deep. i wade through it but suddenly i sink in the mud. elias pulls me out.

sophie is the first to say she's ready to tell me what she remembers. elias doesn't want to. he doesn't want to think about it, he says. and he also is against our returning to thailand. later he does talk to me. but the fact that we want to go back to thailand is beyond his comprehension.

34

as we sat on our mats in the buddhist temple complex – which in all probability was wat sai thai – and deliberated about what to do next, a german fellow came into the hall. he was the owner of a diving school in krabi and had registered with the relief organization care as a volunteer. he had been told to go to all places in the area around krabi where it was known that people were being sheltered, to ascertain what supplies they would need.

edith told him that all we needed was a chance to use a telephone so that we could organize our return trip. theoretically, he said, we could phone from his office, but unfortunately he couldn't take us there. he was on the road with his motorbike and had to visit a few more refugees' quarters. he would see what he could do and come back in the evening. then he spoke with the six others in the hall and drove off again.

because it was just too monotonous to sit and wait for nighttime, we got up again and took a walk through the monastery complex. this time we went past the temple area and came to the modest little houses of the monks and nuns. the most striking thing was the constant howling and barking. in this monastery not only people found shelter, but also dogs and cats, of which the latter had to claim and defend their territory. wild chases and conflicts flared up constantly.

several monks sat in front of their little houses, or, more

accurately, huts. for the most part they were in wretched condition. each in his own way, the monks sat enjoying the balmy evening. they greeted us as we went by. one was even smoking, which indicated that the monastic rules here weren't particularly strict. he offered us cigarettes, and we got into conversation with him. when the cats weren't screeching or racing past the little house, everything was very peaceful here. i asked the monk if this were a mixed monastery. he said that there were nuns here too, but the cardinal rule was that there be no physical contact between men and women.

it had gotten dark as we spoke. a gong struck several times, which the cats and dogs answered with wild howling. the monks left their houses and thronged to a central building, in which there was apparently a meditation room. we went back to our hall. the path was very poorly lighted, and we had a hard time finding our accommodations again.

elias said, he wouldn't mind staying here a little while longer. and then he added: maybe someday i'll become a buddhist monk.

in the hall we sat down on our mats. in the middle of the room stood plastic bottles of drinking water. the English-woman near us was having a hard time. she stared straight ahead, groaned occasionally, and kept moving her legs. i brought her water and offered her pain-killers. she didn't need them, because she too had been given medications at the hospital in krabi. they were in a little plastic bag just like mine.

that reminded me that it was time for me to take my antibiotics. this evening one more tablet, and then three times a day, the doctor had said. this morning on phi phi island we had fled from another potential wave. now we were clearly safe. the worst was over. i could take pills, i could do something to improve my condition. the englishwoman said that the british consulate knew her whereabouts and someone would come for her tomorrow. and we hoped that the german diving business owner would come back and give us more help.

the room was so large that we had virtually no contact with the five people along the opposite wall. the family was busy getting the child to sleep. elias began to read his buddhism book. i positioned myself at the window and thought, despite the continual whirring of the fans and yowling of the animals, i could hear monks chanting in the distance.

in this room you could turn the lights off but not the fans. they had some central control, but i didn't find it. their whirring had anything but a calming effect on us, and their breeze was so strong that we were chilly. to make our bedding softer, we had laid the bath towels on the raffia mats, now we covered ourselves with them. but we couldn't sleep. edith had the most uncomfortable spot of all of us. she said, we're condemned to do nothing; we have get out of here as soon as possible.

after a while two women came into the room. starting with the wall across from us, distributing blankets. then they came to us. they worked for care. i asked: are you by chance driving to krabi?

only one of them spoke english. when she said yes, i asked her if she could take us to the maritime hotel, and she said she would. we packed up our bath towels. downstairs we ran into the german diving school owner. he had come back to us on his motorbike and could explain the directions to the maritime hotel to the two women. we squeezed ourselves, all four of us, into the back seat of a station wagon, in whose cargo space blankets and water bottles were stacked up.

and so we arrived at this big hotel that stands in the middle of the city. its management had decided after the catastrophe, to place all of its infrastructure, as far as possible, at the disposal of everyone who had no shelter. corridors and rooms were filled with injured and desperate people, many of whom had lost family members. here there was a concentration of misery and in our dazed condition we got a chance to see with our own eyes how fortunate we should feel, yet the misery here was being overseen by professionals, and that gave us some hope. part of the lobby had been transformed into a first aid station. there were already embassy or consulate representatives here from several countries – israel, switzerland and australia – there were telephones and a fax machine, and two thai policemen who, assisted by multilingual helpers, registered the stranded people and made lists of the missing. and in the banquet and dining rooms, where mats had been spread out, large tv screens broadcast cnn reports. finally we discovered what the world had known for quite a while.

volunteers staffing an information booth were able to find the telephone number of the austrian embassy in bangkok. then i got in line at one of the telephones. by then it was after 11 p. m. but i telephoned anyway. a woman answered, whose name i couldn't understand correctly despite the fact that i asked several times. i briefly described our situation to her and asked her whether she could give me any advice about how to proceed. she said i was the first austrian to get in touch from krabi. she wanted to know whether there were other austrians there, which i couldn't say. she was of the opinion that we should try to get to phuket on our own, where there were a lot of other austrians, and an honorary consul in charge of them. she gave me a telephone number.

people warned me against traveling to phuket because they said the chaos was much worse there, and no one could tell me how to get there without any money, i decided to telephone the honorary consul there, but his telephone line was always busy.

a woman working for the swiss embassy told us that thai airways were offering tourists who had lost everything free flights to bangkok. i wrote a fax to the austrian embassy in bangkok, in which i informed them that we would try to get to bangkok the next day with thai airways.

before we received valium from the doctor and i made my way to the hotel bar, i inquired at the information booth whether there was a list of patients from the hospital in krabi from which one might tell whether austrians had been treated there. the woman promised me she would make inquiries.

the next morning, quite early, the list was posted. it was fourteen pages long. i picked out the austrians and wrote a further fax to the embassy including the names of the eleven austrians who had been treated the day before in the hospital in krabi. then i made my way into the city to the office of thai airways. i was very lucky that the office was right nearby. but it was still closed. i waited for the first employee to arrive. she told me that the refugees, which is what we were being called now, were being given seats on a standby basis right at the airport. i limped back to the hotel, woke up the children in the dining room – edith had already gone to the bathroom to wash up – and ten minutes later we were sitting in the hotel minibus, which took us, along with a couple of regular passengers, to the krabi airport. during the trip, elias scooped clean several packets of jelly. he had taken them from the buffet that had been set up by the hotel employees for the occupants of the dining room. the jelly packets obviously didn't taste of decay.

35

on the last day of our second trip to phi phi island we meet a slender, blue-eyed man with long blonde hair on the bay directly below our bungalow. he's playing diabolo on the beach and greets us cordially. he has mastered this game superbly and with it, so he tells us, earned considerable pocket money on the beaches of east asia. his name is ernst and he comes from bremen. he has been traveling for fourteen months. when he started his trip, all he had was money for his flight to australia. there he survived on odd jobs, shipped aboard a sailboat, and traveled on to indonesia. it is his ambition to return to bremen without using an airplane. but not right away. not until it's warmed up again at home.

he's met a lot of people who have traveled around the world on their parents' money, he tells us. he despises that.

he'd like to be an author most of all. he'd have a lot to tell. it
soon becomes evident that, in a way, he's been one for a long
time. he hosts a website where he posts entries about his
travels whenever he finds an internet café. he wants to stay on
phi phi island over christmas and travel on the mainland later.

we wish him good luck and cross over to lohdalum bay to
visit the phi phi tsunami memorial park on our last day on the
island. it is located right at the foot of the phi phi viewpoint
resort, almost at sea level. the paklong bungalows used to
stand here, but no trace of them remains. it is strange that this
memorial spot has been planned for merely one season. the
botanical garden planned here, about twenty by thirty meters
in size, will embody both the memory of that which is
transitory and the transitory nature of memory. even a small
tidal wave could wash it away. it's supposed to be finished on
december 26th for the second anniversary of the catastrophe.

several thai workers are moving around with wheelbarrows
and shovels, transporting flagstones for paths. flowers, bushes,
and trees are being planted. flower beds are being built, and
benches placed, in the middle of all this. in contrast to most of
the other construction sites around, the materials here are
stacked in orderly piles. even the empty cement bags have been
neatly piled. the park is being established with contributions.
little stone tablets with the names of the deceased will
memorialize the people who lost their lives in the tsunami. on
a website, tourists are asked to give money for these memorial
tablets to the thai dead whose family members can't afford
them. the tsunami memorial park is very close to a recently
constructed cement tower on which several sirens are
mounted. in case of a new tsunami, these are supposed to warn
the people on phi phi island in time.

we sit down on one of the new benches, already sensing
our immanent departure. the bushes all around us are in
bloom. the first memorial stones lie there under a tarpaulin.
will they be laid out along the path or set into a wall, like the
vietnam memorial in washington? our names will not be

among them. it was the correct decision to return. phi phi island is now more than just the island of terror in our memory. it was also good to experience how deeply the people who live here love their island.

the inhabitants have found their way back to their lives, and the phi phi tsunami memorial park will soon disappear again. we assume that this time our departure will not be chaotic, that it will take place the way we have planned and booked it. tomorrow we shall fly to munich and spend one night in a hotel. i have a meeting the next day, and then we'll drive back to vienna by car. we foresee no further catastrophes. it is our way of coming to terms with the ephemeral nature of life.

at our previous departure it was completely uncertain exactly how and when things would proceed. we spent the whole day at krabi airport. we certainly weren't the only people without money or tickets who wanted to get away. the airport police distributed temporary identity papers for the airline and border control. at the thai airways counter our names were put on a standby list. we were told our names would be called, as soon as there were seats on a plane for bangkok. planes were continually flying to bangkok. at some point i noticed people checking in who had clearly registered at the standby counter after us. that was when i understood the system. you had to put yourself down on a new list for each airplane. i spent the whole day at the thai airways standby counter. when it was my turn i stood at the end of the line again, aside from giving precedence to those who couldn't walk and those who were more badly injured, it wasn't quite clear what criteria were being used to assign seats.

edith and the children for the most part just sat around, either in the departure hall or outside under the palm trees. elias read the book on buddhism that he had taken from the roof of the phi phi hotel. he asked a man who sat beside us smoking for a cigarette, and the man immediately handed him a whole pack of marlboros. he was dead drunk. he kept clapping elias on the shoulder and laughing. on the one hand elias was glad the man was being so nice to him, but on the other he was a little intimidated. he told me about him when we left the airport building to go out for a cigarette break.

when we came back i asked him to show me the man – and i recognized him. i had talked to him the night before in the maritime hotel. he was a swede. he told me that he had lost his family, his wife and his son. we sat down beside him. he said he was also waiting for a flight to bangkok. and from there he wanted to continue on to stockholm. but a short time later, he said he would stay in thailand. he didn't know what he would do alone at home.

edith and sophie came in and walked up to us, beaming. they had been looking for us. a dutch couple, who hadn't suffered any loss, but was merely travelling home ahead of schedule, had given them a thousand baht, with the instructions to buy ourselves a proper breakfast.

we sat down in the airport restaurant, suddenly overwhelmed with luxury. we ate and drank – coffee, toast, jam, eggs, croissants, everything we could get for a thousand baht.

later, as i was doing my rounds again at the standby counter, a french journalist spoke to edith. she wanted details about our situation. at the end of the conversation she opened her suitcase and took out some long slacks and gave them to her. she said, for your arrival back home in winter.

our names were called at six p. m., after a long day of waiting. we boarded the plane to bangkok. during the flight copies of the bangkok post, a thai newspaper in english, were distributed. the title page showed an aerial photograph of the destruction on koh phi phi.

elias happened to be sitting next to the swede who had given him the pack of marlboros. he ordered one whiskey after another. he told elias that he had a harley he liked to ride at home. it sounded as though he were going to head back to sweden after all. in the meantime, elias kept reading in the buddhism book. the swede, who by this time, smelled strongly of alcohol, showed some interest in it. he wanted to buy it from him. elias gave it to him as a present. the swede thanked him effusively and began to leaf through it himself. after a few more drinks, served to him without question, he fell asleep. in bangkok the swede disappeared. he didn't enter the airport terminal where the officials of the individual countries had set up shop to assist their citizens with their homeward journeys. i told the swedish authorities about this man, but they couldn't find him anywhere.

in the airport first aid station we received treatment again. in the process i witnessed a remarkable scene, in which a nurse implored elias for forgiveness for the tsunami. as though this act of nature had been her fault. she all but begged him to come back to thailand and didn't calm down until he promised.

edith's brother, burkhard, my brother stefan and his girlfriend, brit, all picked us up at the airport. they brought warm clothing and a thermos bottle of tea. that was helpful because, for whatever reason, we had landed far from the terminal. as we waited in the transfer bus, we had been freezing, with the doors open, in minus zero temperature. most of the pasengers had all of their clothing. only a few of them, who had come without tickets, arrived in shorts and t-shirts. in the airport terminal itself we then went through a room where the red cross offered us clothing.

our own car was parked outside in the parking lot, of course, but we no longer had a key for it. our brothers had come in two cars to accommodate all of us. they had gotten the last existing apartment key from teresa, who cleans for us once a week. my brother stefan gave us fifty euros, and with it we bought baked goods, ham and eggs from the butcher in our building. we all had breakfast together and then opened a bottle of champagne. after the hugs and champagne drinking, and then more hugs, they took us to the lorenz-böhler hospital.

36

so the east has let you out again, the butcher greets me. he stands beside his refrigerated trailer, i've just come from the night train, i'm unshaven and, as i can see in the windshield, my hair is plastered down. four months ago the butcher was on crutches. both his knees were operated on. now he's carrying half a calf on one shoulder. i pick up my pace, pull the key out of my pocket and push open the outer door. the butcher squeezes through the doorway with the calf. after a couple of steps he turns around. one of the calf's hind hooves scrapes along the mailboxes. the butcher's face has dark red patches from the exertion. droplets fall from the calf's neck. the head has been removed.

how's the hand? asks the butcher. i show him the blue plastic splint that encases my left arm from fingers to elbow. incredible says the butcher. then he lets the hoof scrape along the mailboxes again and goes up a couple of stairs with the calf. you'll be fine, herr doctor, he calls into the empty, echoing stairwell, before he disappears around the corner. i hear him open the iron door to the mysterious room, from which i can sometimes hear the sound of the bone saw. the calf has left a trail of bloody water on the floor behind it.

edith hugs me for a long time. she says, you should have stayed here. why do you have to go back to work?

i want to lead a normal life, i say.

what is normal? she asks.

for me, it's normal to drive away and come home again.

a man telephoned, she says, from the central lost and found service. a few moldy things have apparently arrived from thailand. he asked if he should just toss them out, or if

we wanted them. i said we wanted to throw them away ourselves.

that's good, i say. what is it?

don't know. he says everything is useless, stinking, kaput.

she leans against me. i embrace her. good that you're here,
she says.

the central lost and found service is housed on the third
floor of the semmelweis clinic. the walls of the freight elevator
are paneled in that corrugated aluminum that used to be a big
hit as an east german export. over decades of transporting
hospital beds, the once ochre-colored panels are now scraped
and battered. there's a note stuck up beside the buttons. the
preschool on the top floor requests that you not block the
elevator. i imagine kindergarten teachers carrying unconscious
children downstairs in their arms. at every landing they gather
by the elevator door and bang on it before they keep running
down.

in the long, vaulted corridor the hanging globes are lit all
day. on one of the doors there's a sign with the clearly visible
wording, business hours. i expected a lot of people, but there is
no one here. just an empty bench for three or four people.
since, according to the sign, it's still office hours, i knock and
open the door. the former hospital ward is dominated by two
desk fortresses. one of them is opposite the door unoccupied.
behind the other sits a young, dark-haired man, smoking. a
second man with a large ring in his ear, has flopped down on
one of the nearby tables. both look over at us. i give my name
and say that we got a phone call.

yes, says the man behind the desk. of the two, it's obvious
that he is the official civil servant here. yes, he says, so you've
come. you can look at the stuff and take it with you, if you
want it.

he stubs out his cigarette and walks over to some high
shelves. the other man skulks off to the corner by the window
and looks out. he seems embarrassed, as though he were here

on private business and, now that, surprisingly, clients have come out of the blue, he doesn't know quite what to do. after a while he slinks out through a door into the next room without saying goodbye. maybe his desk is there.

the official taking care of us is friendly. he brings out a cardboard box and puts it on the table. on the box is a picture of a baby buddha, colored purple, who holds a bottle that is much too big for his hands. the buddha has a faux hawk hairdo. thai writing frames the picture. a red label says what it used to contain: soy sauce, healthy boy brand.

there you go, says the official. he opens the lid and steps back a bit. inside the box top someone has written austrian in felt-tipped pen. a foul stench pours out. we step a little closer. edith's moldy wallet is visible, a wet passport impregnated with sand, airline tickets stuck together, a soggy strap. i pull on it and my camera bag appears. it looks like a wrung-out sock, which somebody has dropped in a puddle on the way to the clothesline. i push the airline tickets aside. it stinks. underneath lie the digital camera, cell phones, credit cards, a keychain with encrusted keys, everything damp and stuck together with sand. obviously the contents of our waterlogged bungalow safe have been delivered to vienna. an envelope is attached to the side of the carton. the official pulls it out.

i have already looked at this, he says. there's thai money inside. the national bank will probably exchange it for you.

i glance inside the envelope. it contains damp, brown-spotted baht notes, held together by a rusty paperclip.

you can leave the rest here, the official says.

i look at edith and edith looks at me. we'll take the box with us, she says.

fine with me, says the official. just sign here to confirm receipt for me. he puts a piece of paper in front of me. it says that the personal items listed below were conveyed to the austrian officials by kurt sutherland, an employee of the british consulate. i sign. he puts a second form in front of me, listing in thirty-eight bullet points the contents of the package:

passports, film cassettes, drivers' licenses, bank cards, even the customer cards from jacques's wine warehouse and the reader's card from the leipzig university library are listed. there you go, says the official, and makes a note on the list, objects received on february 11, 2005, and i sign.

there's one more envelope, says the official, and walks to a bookcase. haslinger, elias. part of your group?

that's our son, i say.

he brings us the envelope. it is still sealed. the official opens it with scissors. he says, look at that. there are euro notes inside.

we confirm the receipt of this envelope. it holds the contents of our children's safe. it isn't much. elias, who had refused to let the safe be opened, was now getting his money back. we had put the christmas letters from oma, opa, and aunt anni in our safe. they had contained euro notes. the euro notes from our safe were missing.

back home i begin to clean out the carton and put the contents on the radiator. but the stench gets so strong that i pack everything up again. it smells like mold and sewers, it smells like the green iowa t-shirt and the shorts that dried on my body.

edith flings the window open. she asks: did we really have much cash with us?

yes, i say. i wanted to be on the safe side.

she says, you can't hold it against the thais.

no, i said, you can't.

i take the box to my office, turn the radiator up to the highest setting and open the window. i put printer paper on the floor. then i take the objects out of the box one at a time, carefully shake out the sand, and lay them out to dry. i put the soaked tickets and documents directly on the radiator. at the bottom of the box lie the encrusted keys and coins, about which it is impossible to tell if they're european or asian. they look like they come from the roman period. with a screwdriver i try to clean the blade of a key. the crust is as good as welded on. then i get an idea. i fill a pot with vinegar and throw all the coins and keys into it. after a while i stir it thoroughly with a screwdriver and empty the liquid into the toilet. coins and keys are now cleaned. of course they've now taken on a uniform red tinge. you can't tell any longer whether the coins are gold or silver. i take one of these red keys and try it in the office door. it works.

sand has accumulated in the bottom of the box. i go to the sink, put the box on the edge, and begin to empty out the sand. it soon forms a little pointed mountain at the drain, from which small bits break off and roll down. i take one of the pieces and crumble it and smell my fingers. in the cupboard under the sink i find an empty jelly glass. i spoon part of the sand into it. when i want to go on emptying the box i notice that a piece of paper has come loose from the bottom. it is folded. i open it. at the top i read pp phi phi princess resort, and under that haslinger, sosef (sic!), edith as well as the nationality, austria. and after that: valuables. five bullet points list our valuables, even the bank notes in baht and euros. we received the baht notes in the precise amount recorded.

it's only now that it occurs to me to visit the website of our former hotel. the homepage begins with a long condolence note to all family members. the reconstruction of the hotel is announced, perhaps with a somewhat bad conscience, because the text contains the following wording: anyone who has the knowledge of construction that can resist the tsunami tidal wave or any suggestions for our reconstruction, kindly send to us via our e-mail.

a link takes you to the guest list of december 26. beside the names it says either safe at home, missing, or died. Next to my name it says safe at home. alexander osang told me that he had verified that with the hotel management. it says missing next to edith, elias, and sophie's names. i write an e-mail to the contact address listed there. within a half-hour i get an answer. the webmaster thanks me. he says he has updated the list. i check it. now we are all safe at home. i look for claude and emine. it says missing for both of them. i write another e-mail to thailand. emine and i took the same boat to krabi, so i know she's alive. but she probably could have reported that herself. the note missing remains next to her name.

the hotel website also says that the safes they recovered had been opened and their contents given to the british embassy. i get off the net.

the box with the baby buddha is still lying in the sink. i turn it over and knock the remaining sand out of it. i hear a clinking sound. a hidden coin, i think. but it isn't a coin, it's a medal of the virgin mary. my mother gave it to me a long time ago. she knew that i would never put it around my neck, and so she asked me to carry it in my wallet. she said it would protect me. now the metal has deteriorated. the inscription on the border has become illegible. but i know what it used to say.

the next day we are invited to visit our friends, bigi and helmut. bigi works for radio austria. i say that along with the stench from the contents of the safes, the images have caught up with us again too. i say that nature does not differentiate between a human being and a camera bag. i drink a lot this evening. later i wonder: why didn't whoever helped himself to our euro notes take the baht notes, which he could have used just as easily?

because he wasn't in thailand, says bigi.

in the morning she calls me up and says, you'll get your money back.

you're joking, i say.

no, she says. i phoned the central lost and found service and said i was researching the case and mentioned incidentally that i was in contact with you. i told the official he should call me when he had discovered something about the whereabouts of your money. and now, not an hour later, he's phoned to say another envelope has turned up – with your money.

shortly after that i get a call from the official. he says he has good news for us. i don't say that i already know.

when edith comes home from work, we drive back to the semmelweis clinic. now the second desk fortress is occupied. there sits a blonde, with a ring on every finger. she is texting on her cell phone with astonishingly long nails. she pays no attention to us. our official fusses all the more. he shakes our hands and keeps saying, there you go. he picks up a list. there you go, he says, and leads us to another room, but can't open the door. he has to run back to get a new key, and he says: there you go, unlocks the door, takes a different key from his pocket, there you go, unlocks a cupboard, takes out an envelope, a new envelope, with no writing on it: there you go. i am expecting stained euro notes stuck together with sand. the official says, there you go, and counts fresh bank notes onto the table. precisely the amount that was on the list that lay at the bottom of the box.

that can't be our money, i say. our money was in the same safe as the other things.

a small service, he says. i exchanged the money for new bills at the national bank.

you've been to the national bank?

not in person, he says. i sent an assistant.

i thank him. we walk back into the other office. he puts a sheet of paper in front of me. there you go, he says. if you would please sign this. the sheet meticulously lists all the sums of money that had been found in our wallets, divided into baht and euros. i ask the official to make copies of everything i have signed. he retrieves the file from his desk. he doesn't seem to know how to work the copier. the woman with the long fingernails is still paying no attention to us. she keeps texting on her cell phone. through the window behind her, i can see that it has started to snow heavily.

there you go. the official has finished the copies. i thank him and glance through them. the page that i have just signed is nothing more than the continuation of the list from last time. in addition to a listing of our cash, down to the last cent, it contains objects that were found in the baby buddha box, the keys for example. at the end it says: austrian consulate phuket, January 24, 2005.

i want to shake the official's hand as i leave, but he has already retreated behind his desk fortress. good-bye, i say. yes, 'bye, he says, without looking at us.

the bastiengasse now looks like the approach to a ski jump. two cars have stopped, as if they don't dare to drive down it.

we meet the butcher on the stairs of our building. he's carrying a plastic tub.

hullo, herr doctor, he says, would you like some spicy sausages?

with pleasure, i say.

he puts the tub on the floor and hangs a string of paprika sausages over the handrail. it's gonna be alright, he says.

what do i owe you? i ask.

that's okay, herr doctor.

i thank him.

at home i hand our children their christmas presents from oma, opa, and aunt anni for the second time. there you go, i say, as i distribute the fifties. there you go, and there you go, and there you go. and then i put a sausage on top of each bill.

37

while working on this report i found a website that gave information about the fate of emine's friend, claude. it took a long time until his body was found and could be identified by his daughter valentine. on the website thaicareyou.com, the main portal for tsunami victims in thailand, his file could finally be closed on may 21, 2005. valentine expresses her thanks for the help of volunteer workers, for the condolence messages, and the memorial candles that had been posted on her father's page on the website.

internet research on emine revealed that after we separated

she was apparently brought to phuket and treated there in a hospital. then her trail disappears. on august 8, 2005, emine was still reported as missing on thaihaynes.com, the central listing of tsunami victims in thailand. that surprised me, and i made several attempts to establish contact with her, none of which succeeded. then a year later, on august 6, 2006, i stumbled onto a website where i found the information that she had taken part in a women's 145 kilometer run and come in eleventh.

Afterword
by
Thomas S. Hansen

Born in Zwettl, Lower Austria, in 1955, Josef Haslinger studied philosophy, theater, and German Studies in Vienna where he received his Ph.D. in 1980 with a dissertation on the aesthetics of the Romantic poet Novalis. This background prepared him for a broad spectrum of literary activity that includes journalism, literary criticism, and fiction writing. Haslinger's academic career reflects his multifaceted literary training, experience, and talents. He has held guest lectureships at several universities. While at the university of Kassel in 1995, for example, he wrote parts of his very successful novel, *Opernball* (S. Fischer Verlag, 1995). This political thriller depicts a Neo-Nazi terrorist attack on the waltz cotillion that is Vienna's most elegant annual social event. Translated into several languages and made into a television film in 1998, *Opernball* expanded Haslinger's fame beyond the borders of Austria. Ironically, the plot contains an eerie adumbration of his real experience in *Tsunami. A Report from Phi Phi Island.* The protagonist in *Opernball* (a journalist filming the live television coverage of the ball) watches the crime unfold on his monitors, including his teenaged son's death, when the boy, a cameraman at the ball, inhales the poison gas that kills most of the other participants. The same situation confronts Haslinger during the tsunami in reality on Phi Phi Island, when as grieving parents the author and his wife think they may have lost their eighteen-year-old twins, Sophie and Elias, to the tsunami.

Since 1996 Haslinger has held a professorship in literary aesthetics at the German Literary Institute in Leipzig. In many of his works he fixes a powerful critical gaze on Austrian social realities, challenging his readers to confront controversial aspects of the history and social conventions of his homeland. He has also written critically about the USA. His intellectual perspective and observations have won him many distinguished prizes in contemporary Austrian letters.

Tsunami. A Report from Phi Phi Island takes readers through the family's fateful choice of their Christmas holiday destination: Thailand rather than Jamaica, because of the appeal of cheap air fares and tropical beaches. He explains that the trip is a pre-graduation present for their twins, now in their last year of school. To these Viennese, Thailand seems a dream destination for a beach vacation during the chilly northern winter, so on a friend's recommendation they settle on exotic Phi Phi Island with its magnificent coast, wild youth scene, and choices of either luxury or austere accommodations.

Since Haslinger wrote this report of the catastrophe in Thailand, the globe has suffered more devastation from earthquakes and the tsunamis they can cause. In a sense, Haslinger's account of his experience is still timely – perhaps timeless – reading. He did not begin this remarkable firsthand memoir until a year-and-a-half after the event, which the trauma – both acknowledged and unconscious – had blocked him from facing. His first literary decision was not to displace experience in the guise of literary fiction, which would have necessitated a surrogate protagonist to represent his emotions. Instead, Haslinger tells his story as straightforward reportage and checks his recollections against reality by returning to the island where he and his family nearly died.

Phi Phi Island is Haslinger's first major work to appear in English, and while its straightforward narrative style is very readable, it does pose several questions about literary form. To begin with, the author's own subtitle, "A Report," announces an approach to his tale of suffering and catastrophe that suggests objectivity. Yet, the reader will find more here than a factual reportage of the harrowing experiences of Christmas 2004. While the family members all escaped with only minor injuries, the tsunami haunts them on their return home to Vienna. Bad dreams, problems in school, panic attacks – all point to unresolved symptoms resembling post-traumatic stress disorder, which threatens to damage their lives. When Haslinger, who thought himself the strongest member of the family and least likely to suffer psychological aftershocks, finds himself ducking for cover in central Vienna and suffering tormenting dreams, he decides to exorcize his lingering fears by returning to the scene a year after the tsunami in order to confront the past at the spot where he and his family nearly suffered the fate of thousands of others. This second trip – for research, not relaxation – grafts later personal experience onto the historical core of the work, which is Haslinger's original memory of the tsunami itself.

Haslinger's narrative of the former tourist paradise thus unfolds on two levels as he walks familiar ground, surveys the devastation, recalls the horrors of the deadly event, and tries to reconstruct his memories. This device, which interweaves memory with the process of recovering these memories, brings a dynamic to the tale that transcends straightforward chronological reportage.

Upon opening the book, the reader is immediately struck by its unique visual impact: the entire text printed in lower case type – an extraordinary eccentricity, because in the German language, nouns are capitalized. But not in this book where the lower-case narrative is no affectation but a necessity for Haslinger who suffered severed tendons in the third and fourth fingers in his left hand during the tsunami. The little finger, essential for typing capital letters on a keyboard, he humorously calls his "tsunami finger." This injury produces the visual device that seems to project some avant-garde intention, whereas it is actually reminding readers of the physical (and psychological) disability behind this prose. Thus, the very face of the printed page visually declares the pain that the narrative captures in language.

Haslinger's report is the first serious literary treatment of this natural catastrophe that claimed the lives of over 200,000 people on the rim of the Indian Ocean. To be sure, there are several works of journalism that describe the events of the earthquake and the tsunami of 2004, including a great deal of amateur film footage. Several pictorial accounts and treatments for juvenile readers exist as well. Yet, with *Tsunami. A Report from Phi Phi Island* Haslinger has embarked on an ambitious work of creative non-fiction. This form of writing exists between the purely fictional realm of the imagination and the journalistic world of attempted objectivity. Such texts deal with both verifiable fact and experienced truth. Yet, while content can be checked and the first-person narrator held accountable for reliability, not even a work like this in which the narrator's voice is always loud and clear, can claim complete objectivity.

Haslinger's narrative voice mediates his own life experience, projecting the fear, hope, and pain of those terrible hours when he encounters corpses of tourists he recognizes, comforts wounded strangers, aids new acquaintances, or believes his children may be among the dead. His harrowing narrative names individuals and traces their fates. He describes the destruction of property and wildlife, the survivors' responses, sparing nothing including the harrowing task of separating the corpses from the living. The report ruminates on the power of chance, that random pattern that saved him and his family. He uses the words "final judgment" ironically, because the implacable and impartial force of the tsunami neither spared the innocent nor punished the guilty. And this difference between fiction, where a protagonist can identify and punish the guilty, and fact, where by chance people are stunned and powerless, is not lost on Haslinger. He and his wife are purely lucky to be reunited with their children, whose own first-person accounts he includes. Even while remaining true to the authenticity of the event, a participant cannot help but refract experience with painful subjectivity.

For Josef Haslinger, the very act of writing produces the cure for the effects of the trauma he memorializes. The language of psychology calls his condition post-traumatic stress syndrome and the act of confronting it, exposure therapy. This refers to a process that lets patients who are persistently reliving a trauma and producing distress that affects their lives, confront and control their fears by vividly reliving the trauma in a controlled environment. What more detailed confrontation with one's own trauma exists than the introspection of autobiography? By recovering his ordeal in detail, facing facts and remembering specific names, faces, and places, Haslinger turns haunting fear into objective memory and can lay the ghosts of Phi Phi Island to rest.